practical CLASSICS
& CAR RESTORER

FORD 100E
BRIEFING

Published by
KELSEY PUBLISHING LIMITED

Printed in Great Britain by Bayliss Printing
Company Limited, Stanley Street,
Worksop, Nottinghamshire, on behalf of
Kelsey Publishing Ltd, Kelsey House,
High Street, Beckenham, Kent BR3 1AN.
Under licence from EMAP National
Publications Limited.

ISBN 1 873098 19 7

© 1991

Contents

Introduction

It took a long time for the Ford 100E to be accepted as a classic. Out-dated from the moment of its launch, with its sidevalve engine and Ford's stubborn allegiance to their three-speed gearbox, as soon as they aged the 100Es found themselves very much unloved. Even when *Practical Classics* magazine bought one as a project car and staff car only just over eight years ago, there were many readers who protested that it was not a classic and never would be. Some *Practical Classics* staff initially had their reservations and were not adverse to joking about the "flying brick".

However as the months went by it came to occupy a place in our hearts. It was in fact very "driveable" and, by comparison to many other classic cars that had been adopted as staff cars, it was very reliable. Today there are very few people who, on seeing a Ford 100E driving down the road, would fail to recognise it as a classic.

This BRIEFING book is an uprated version of the previous 'mini-book', with more pages added and produced to a higher quality. It will enable us to keep available material from the past pages of *Practical Classics & Car Restorer* that we believe will prove useful and very interesting to the enthusiast.

Gordon Wright

Back cover A proud new owner for the Ford 100E when *Practical Classics* sold it after the project.

NB: Any prices quoted were current only at the time that the original article was written.

Pick of the Price Guide

Ford Prefect 100E

The Prefect was the four-door, slightly better equipped and relatively less numerous variant of Ford UK's 1950's small car. A total of 255,655 were produced between December 1953 and September 1959, the number of two-door Anglias made exceeded this by just over 35%.

The 100E was a completely new car — nothing more than the model names being handed down from its predecessor. Despite the engine having the same cylinder dimensions it too was completely new although a side valve layout was retained for reasons of economy. The new unit had the advantage over previous examples of adjustable tappets, an integral water pump for the thermostatically controlled cooling system and more robust crankshaft and connecting rods — the latter sufficiently so to enable later conversion to shell bearings if desired. Cost dictated that transmission was once again 3-speed, while final drive was by spiral bevel gears. The few mechanical changes during production include an increase from 7″ to 8″ brakes in January 1955, a lower first and second gear from April 1955 and the rarely found option of Newtondrive 2 pedal control for 12 months from October 1957.

Cosmetic changes to trim and light details were made occasionally and on the introduction of a De Luxe version in October 1955, the subsequent 'standard' model was slightly less well equipped. The most noticeable external change came with a face-lift in October 1957 which included a significantly enlarged rear window. The four-door body has obvious advantages of convenience over a two-door, although a little more care must be exercised while navigating through the narrower openings.

Although 100Es have survived in quite large numbers, corrosion in the unitary construction usually determines when the end has arrived. Careful checks should be made of the sills — both inner and outer and all the adjoining box sections. Likewise, rear spring attachment points are vital and the box section over and behind the back axle is prone to disappear.

Engines usually last reasonably well, but tend to fume and smoke after relatively short mileages in some cases — and are less economical than might be imagined. Transmission lasts well although the rear hub bearings run directly in the axle casing resulting in occasional problems. Certain mechanical parts — notably steering and front suspension are proving difficult to find. The increase in demand for certain items has resulted in their remanufacture both by the Ford Sidevalve Club and outside sources.

Engine: 1172cc. Compression ratio 7:1, 36 b.h.p.
Transmission: 3 speed gearbox — optional Newtondrive from October 1956 to October 1957. Spiral bevel final drive — ratio 4.429:1
Performance: Maximum speed 71 m.p.h. Fuel consumption 30 m.p.g.
Weight: 14½ cwt.

FADING FORD?

Put new life into your 100E engine

Joss Joselyn takes you step by step through a Ford 100E engine overhaul.

Tremendously popular in its heyday, the Ford 100E side-valve engine disappeared from the new car scene around twenty years ago. It was fitted to the Anglia and Prefect up to September 1959 and then carried on for a while in the Popular, but the introduction of the overhead valve engined Anglia was the writing on the wall and the 100E, so far as Fords were concerned, was the last of the side-valves.

It is not a difficult engine to overhaul and to find out just what work was involved, I went down to Tipler Engineering, 636 Old Kent Road, London, SE15 where they still work on them regularly and a great many of the important stages can be seen in our comprehensive photo sequence. To start at the very beginning, removing the engine shouldn't give a lot of trouble. It comes out in the traditional manner, through the top of the engine compartment, the gearbox being left in situ, supported on a jack while lifting, and then hung on a wire sling from the bulkhead. Taking the bonnet off makes the job easier but the radiator can be left in, although it might be better to be safe than sorry and have it out.

A Haltrac hoist is ideal for lifting and although the job is often done with a chain attached to a lifting hook screwed in place of one of the headbolts, it can be done just as well with wire slings wrapped around the engine.

Tools you will need

Set of A/F spanners • Engine lifting equipment • Micrometer • Valve compressor • Valve grinding paste • Valve holder with a sucker • Feeler gauges • Torque wrench • Complete gasket set • Piston ring clamp or compressor • Circlip Pliers.

DISMANTLING

When you're working at home, it's a good idea to wash the engine off first. Paint it all over with Gunk or something similar and then swill it off with a hosepipe. It wasn't done in our photographic sequence because all the parts were going straight into a chemical hot wash plant.

Ford use bolts to secure the head rather than the studs that were more popular around that time and this certainly makes head removal easier. There are 14 of them and 5/8in. A/F is the size.

It is worthwhile to get yourself a bit organised before you get into dismantling proper, particularly if you don't know what you're going to find. Just in case you find there isn't a great deal of wear and you want to rebuild using most of the same components, you'll need to keep some of them in order. Keep a bit of space available on the bench or on a sheet of newspaper where you can lay the parts out.

Collect a series of small containers — cardboard boxes, old egg cartons or those foil Indian restaurant containers are ideal. This will help you keep nuts and bolts, washers, spacers, oil throwers and anything together with the main part removed. It helps get bolts back in the right place and prevents you forgetting washers and other bits and pieces. Even write notes if you think it will help.

If you are thinking of an exchange short motor, instead of getting involved in a complete rebuild job yourself, the sump must be the next item to come off. Now, if you have the necessary micrometer etc. you can measure up the wear — at least on bores and big ends. If you don't have the instruments and particularly if you don't have the know-how, it's best to have this done by your local engineering shop.

Depending on what bore measurement reveals there may be several alternatives open to you. If the bores are deeply scored or if there is more than about 0.008 - 0.010in. wear, a rebore to the next oversize is a must. If wear

Start dismantling by slackening the head bolts. Tackle the inner ones first and work out towards the corners. There are five in the middle row don't miss the two adjacent to the top hose stub. Tapping all round with a hammer should free the head. Use a hammer with a soft head or interpose a block of wood. Do not try hammering anything between the head and block.

Now the distributor drive can be lifted out and must be kept safely, particularly if a short motor exchange is called for.

Undo all the ½in. A/F sump bolts right around the flange, tap it free with a soft-headed hammer and lift it off.

Take great care with this alloy oil filter housing. If the engine is humped about with it still in position it can soon get damaged.

Take out the bolts and release the side cover. Knock the tube through so the valve chest breather cap can be taken off for cleaning.

is less than 0.005in., simply fitting new rings might be the answer. Wear up to about 0.010in. can be tackled by fitting oil control rings or better still PEP pistons which are designed to go into worn bores.

However, if the bores and the crankshaft are both worn and, particularly if there has been a recent history of heavy oil consumption and loss of power, an exchange short motor is probably the best answer.

This, for the uninitiated is a completely re-conditioned cylinder block, fitted with a re-ground crankshaft, new main bearing shells, new pistons and re-metalled big ends on the con rods. It also includes re-ground valves, a new timing chain, a camshaft and bearings which have been inspected and replaced if necessary and an oil pump that has been checked over. Exactly what a short motor entails is something you should check with your local reconditioner — there are variations, depending on where you go.

If you opt to master-mind the over-haul yourself, you'll need to continue with the dismantling along the lines shown in the photographs. It is important to mark all the big end caps before you remove them. If you mark the cap and the rod both on the same side with one, two, three or four nicks with a file and later assemble the marks together and on the same side of the engine, you can't go wrong. It should not be possible to get the main bearing caps mixed up.

Fish out the distributor drive as soon as you take the head off and this will ensure you don't lose it, particularly if the engine is going to be exchanged.

Note the position of the distributor drive with the valves on No. 4 rocking which means that No. 1 is on TDC on the firing stroke. You'll need this information when you reassemble in order to get the timing right.

You can, in fact, get the valves out without the use of a spring compressor, provided you have good strong fingers but you might as well use the right tool because you'll need it for rebuilding. Arrange all the valve springs, collets and cam followers with their respective valve and number each assembly so it can be returned to the same place from which it was removed. If, as the professional overhaul man does, you re-grind all the valves and seatings, skim the cam follower surfaces and fit a new set of springs, there's no need to keep them in order.

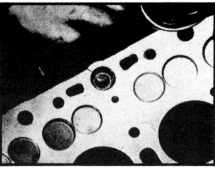

Turn the engine over so that it is on the firing stroke on No. 1 cylinder which is with the valves rocking on No. 4. Note the position and alignment of the distributor drive in its housing. It has been lifted up a little here to make it visible.

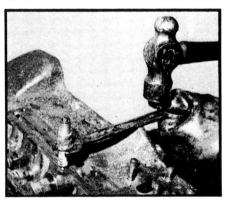

This is the system used to extract the locating plug. A spanner jaw is hooked underneath a sparking plug, the end of which is screwed in. Tapping the end of the spanner will lever it out but be careful or it will fly across the workshop.

Before taking off the big end caps mark both caps and rods so they don't get mixed up.

When all the big end and main bearing caps have been taken off, the crankshaft can be lifted out and the pistons removed through the top of the bore.

Now the compressor is used to squash up the valve springs and a screwdriver tip will fish out the little collets, allowing the valve assemblies to be taken out.

The last item of all to be dismantled is the camshaft which is unlocked and pulled through from the forward end of the block. Cleaning is the next stage and at home it would be done in a bath of cleaning fluid, using a paint brush.

OVERHAUL WORK

If you are going to have the block rebored, it's best to let the reconditioner decide the bore size and depending on whether the engine has been rebored before, he will work to + 0.020in., + 0.030in., + 0.040in., + 0.060in. and in some cases + 0.080in. He is the best person to decide because he will know how much metal has to come out to clean up damage, wear or ovality and he will also know what pistons he has in stock — this is often the limiting factor.

Much the same thing applies to the crankshaft. Usually regrinding is recommended if the main journals are out of round or worn in excess of 0.001in. or the big end crankpins show more than 0.0015in. ovality or wear. Certainly damage in the form of scoring will mean a regrind.

Both with a rebored block and a reground crankshaft, it is much the best plan to get the engine reconditioner to supply the new pistons and the new shell bearings; it cuts down on the possibility of mistakes. Incidentally the main bearing housings on some engines were made 0.015in. oversize. It is vital to check this and fit the correct oversize shell bearings. Ensure

no metal swarf or anything else is left in the oilways. This means swilling cleaning fluid through them and the water jacket.

One more job it might be a good idea to get the reconditioner to carry out is grinding the surface of the cylinder block and the head. Tiplers, if they are doing a short motor or a complete engine, include this as a matter of course but it's a worthwhile extra if you are sorting the overhaul out yourself.

Big ends are something else you cannot really tackle. Re-metalling involves a forge and molten white metal and this, in turn, involves know-how with tinning and fluxes and skill in avoiding air bubbles. All this is followed by accurate machining on the lathe. It's a good idea to ensure that the firm you get to grind your crank can also cope with re-metalling; not every firm has the facilities these days.

When it comes to the valves, much depends on the state they are in. If the engine has been in use a long time, the odds are that you'll have to renew the exhaust valves, although the inlets will probably be in reasonable condition. If there is deep pitting either on the valves themselves or in the seats in the block, professional machining may be required to eliminate it; the same thing applies if the valves have been 'hammering' and there is a lot of damage. The ordinary lapping-in technique will have to be used after serious damage has been machined out.

The cam followers are not susceptible to wear, except after a very long time in use when they develop a depression. The technique here is either to have them re-ground flat or to fit new ones. Check them also to ensure that the valve adjustment thread is not seized and, contrariwise, that the split end to the thread is still intact and the adjuster will still self-lock.

It is no good doing any work on the head or the block if either of them is cracked. Inspect them closely; this is typical of what you might find. If the block is sound, the core plugs should be changed.

When measuring up for wear on the crankpins, both overall wear and ovality will have to be assessed. Unless you are used to using instruments, get the work done by a professional.

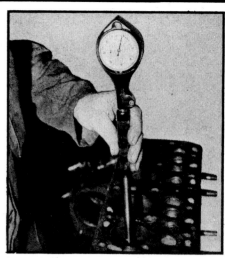

Special instruments and the skill to use them are required to assess bore wear and ovality. Use either an internal micrometer or a bore gauge and dial indicator as here.

If the valves are in good condition cleaning and lapping-in may be adequate. The valves are ground in with grinding paste and a simple valve-holder in the usual way. If the valves are pitted they may need re-grinding on a machine and if the valve seats in the block are pitted or damaged they will have to be re-cut.

Cam followers must be inspected to ensure their surfaces are not wear indented. Check that the adjuster has not seized and that the split end of the thread which is the locking device is still whole.

Re-fitting the valves, springs and collets is best done while the engine is out. A dab of grease will help avoid dropping the collets.

To adjust the valve clearances, you'll need two thin spanners and feeler gauges. The clearance required is 0.012in.

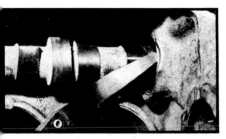

The camshaft on the 100E seldom wears severely and neither does its bearings. Measure bearing wear by inserting feelers. If more than 0.003in. clearance, new bearings will be needed.

ASSEMBLY

Watch a professional engine assembly man at work and you'll see he always seems to have a clean cloth in one hand and an oil can in the other. Everything he builds is first wiped and then oiled.

Cleanliness is particularly vital when assembling bearings, both the shell type used for the mains and the newly metalled big ends. It is also important to get the torque figures right when tightening them. The figure for the mains is 55-60 lb/ft and for the big ends 20-25 lb/ft. Turn the crankshaft before tightening each one to ensure that the previous cap has not locked it.

Most of the important reassembly details can be seen in the photographs. Oil seals are of the fibre type and need trimming after fitting. Ensure they go into scrupulously clean housings and then trim the ends at an angle, high part in the centre.

Thrust washers go at the rear end of the crankshaft, each side of the rear main bearing. The stepped white metal face goes towards the crankshaft (the moving surface) which means they face outwards away from the bearing. The end play should be around 0.002in. measured with feeler gauges.

All new gaskets should be fitted, ensuring they go onto clean dry surfaces. Renew all locking washers too, remembering to bend them up properly to form a proper lock.

Tighten the head bolts down to 65-70 lb/ft observing the correct sequence which goes generally from the centre outwards to the corners. See the diagram on page 10. It is particularly important on this engine because the head does have a tendency to warp.

The oil pump can be checked for wear by inserting feeler gauges between the gear-

wheels and the pump walls; the clearance should be between two and five thou (0.002in. and 0.005in.). Clearance between face of the gears and the cover (measured under a straight-edge) should be between about one and four thou (0.001in. and 0.004in.).

Inspect the oil pressure relief valve which is in the same housing. If the head of the plunger is an unmarked dome, all is well. If it has worn cone shaped, it needs renewal. Lap the plunger into its housing using fine grinding paste or metal polish and fit a new spring.

The remainder of the components go back in the reverse order from dismantling.

The water distribution tube in the block is an item that is best changed.

This coarse woven type of seal is the type mostly used in the 100E, fitted into housings that have previously been cleaned thoroughly.

The seal ends are trimmed with a sharp knife, slicing at the slight angle shown.

New thrust washers are installed with the stepped white metal surface towards the moving faces on the crankshaft.

Clearances are measured and should be no more than 0.002in.

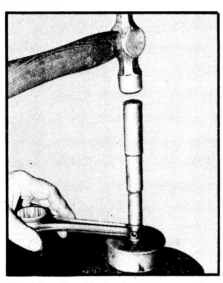

The old small end bushes are driven out using a suitable size mandrel and the new ones are inserted by the same method. Afterwards they should be honed.

If the new pistons are pre-heated in boiling water, it should be possible to push the gudgeon pins home by hand. Do not use force.

Here they are locked into position with internal circlips, inserted using circlip pliers. Check and re-check they are properly positioned.

Always use a proper ring clamp when inserting pistons. These are Hepolite with a skirt ring.

All the main bearings are tightened one at a time and the crankshaft turned to check it is free between each one. Use a torque wrench to get the bolts properly tightened. Follow the same technique with the big ends.

Valve timing is set by lining up marks on the crankshaft sprocket and on the camshaft sprocket. Ignore the dimple on the other side of the camshaft wheel; that's for the E93A engine.

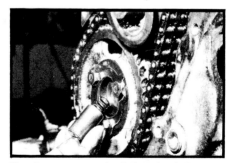

Two items to remember before the timing cover goes on. The crankshaft sprocket oil thrower must go into position and the camshaft plunger which is there to damp out end float. Engine is shown inverted.

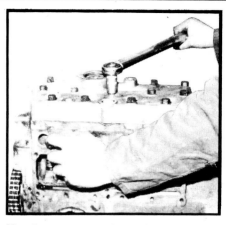

Use the torque wrench to tighten down the headbolts in the approved order, starting in the centre and working out to the corners.

Check the oilpump before fitting. It does not wear badly on this engine, but measure the clearance between sprocket and cover and between gears.

Check the face of the oil pressure relief valve. Wear is indicated by a cone shape; this one is in good condition. Fit a new spring.

There are two fuel pump types on the 100E, one with a longer operating arm than the other. The long-armed one has a thicker gasket and this must be used or rapid cam wear will result.

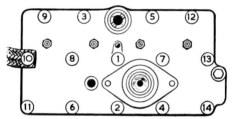

Tightening sequence for cylinder-head nuts.

Back in again — a 100E engine good for many thousands more miles.

A FORD

When are you going to get a Ford? That was the question we kept being asked at shows and by way of readers' letters to the office, and it soon became obvious that Ford owners were beginning to feel that we were ignoring their interests on purpose — at least since we disposed of our workhorse Mk IV Zodiac early this year. But no, we think that old Fords are a vitally important part of the classic car scene and to prove it, we've just bought one to run on our fleet.

Of course, we had a huge variety of elegible vehicles to choose from — anything from a 'Y' type to an RS 2000 would have qualified as being in our field — but in the end we plumped for the humble 100E. Lots of enthusiasts own them, they are powered by the faithful old 1172cc side valve engine used in many other Fords too, and they are still practical for everyday use — because, to make things clear from the start, this isn't going to be an off-the-road restoration project but what we like to call a 'rolling rebuild'. That is, a car in basically good order but requiring a variety of 'weekend' jobs to bring it up to peak condition.

So, having chosen which Ford, how to find one? Not too difficult really, as they still crop up in the local paper, and we generally get at least three or four advertised every month in our own classified pages — and that's how we found XLF 524, scheduled for insertion in our November issue, and advertised at £450 by a Mr Evans from a Canning Town address. In Ford yellow, original and complete with sunvisor, it sounded very hopeful, so off I went to Mr Evans' transport business near the Blackwall Tunnel.

Luckily (it certainly doesn't always follow) the car was as described, and while there were obvious signs of repairs to the lower outer panels, a close examination of the bodywork and underside (greatly assisted by the use of a pit) revealed that the metalwork was in remarkably fine order with apparently not one inch of rot underneath. The interior was slightly grubby but completely unworn, and a trip round the block showed that although the brakes were binding, the engine, gearbox, steering and suspension were sound. Spares included lights, radiator, instruments and other useful bits and pieces so it didn't take long for me to strike a deal at £425 all-in. We had become the proud owners of a 1959 100E!

Mind you, XLF did manage to blot its copybook at the very start — it boiled on the way home when Gordon Wright collected it, indicating that the cooling system as well as the brakes were the first candidates for our attention. But we wanted to get to know the car better anyway, so in conjunction with our friendly mechanic Ted Landon, we gave it a careful inspection.

Fortunately Ted knows the 100E very well having run a couple himself in the past, and

JOINS THE FLEET!

Paul Skilleter describes how we found and evaluated a 100E Prefect, to be run and maintained as a 'Practical Classics' staff car.

we soon had XLF summed-up; as anticipated, the car is in generally excellent original condition, the seized brakes being due to recent lack of use (according to the MoT certificates, it only covered 262 miles in the last year — it was bought from the original

A road-test revealed slightly weak synchro on 2nd but no more than the typical amount of gearbox noise; clutch was judder-free and the suspension felt taut.

A FORD JOINS THE FLEET!

Two-tone interior was excellent, and all instruments except trip worked, even the ammeter on supplementary panel (right of column). Spot and reversing lights worked too. Organ throtle pedal is non-standard.

Seats, door trims and headlining were all perfect; early-type belts had been fitted, and we wonder if those brackets on the front seats are anything to do with them.

owner, a Mr Gane, for Gerald Evans' daughter, but she failed to get on with the three-speed box and so the car was put into storage for a year). The overheating is, we suspect, due to a choked radiator and so we'll be fitting the used spare to see if it makes any difference — so that and new wheel cylinders are the priority jobs.

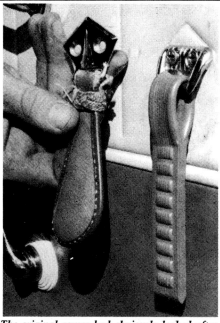

The original owner had obviously looked after the car — tatty door pulls had been replaced but the originals were left in the boot, so we can re-trim and replace them eventually.

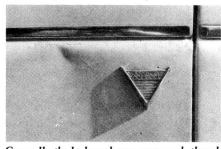

Generally the bodywork was very good, though the odd dent needs to be taken out — as on the nearside front wing and . . .

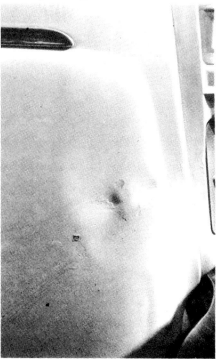

. . . near the tail-light cluster on the offside rear wing.

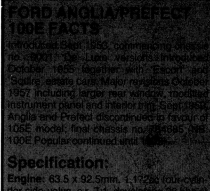

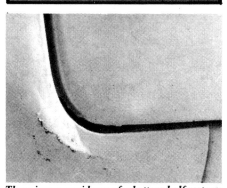

There is some evidence of a bottom-half respray disguising some typical rust areas, such as the bottoms of the front wings near the sills — this is the offside.

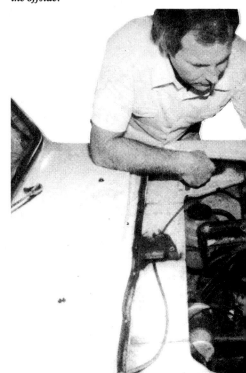

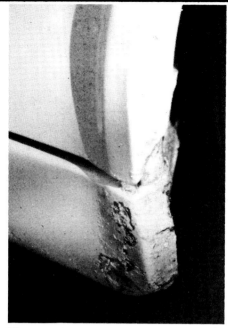

The rear ends of the sills have also gone, but we'll be rectifying the rust over the next few issues with the use of repair panels via the Ford Sidevalve Owners Club.

Engine appears very sound though fumes from breather support the 70,000 miles on the clock. Overheating seems to be the only problem to be cured here, by replacing thermostat and radiator.

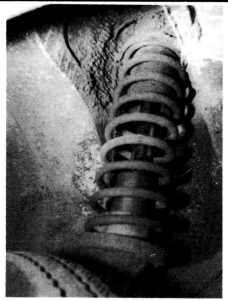

Condition of front struts was checked by 'bouncing' car and by looking for leaks; ours were OK. Unlike other Fords, strut mountings often escape rust on 100Es.

Other front suspension wear point is the lower trunnion, checked for excessive play by levering as shown. The ball joints on XLF appeared very good.

Condition of fluid is often a pointer to state of the hydraulics (brake and clutch) — XLF's was nice and clean.

Front offside brake was binding badly, and adjuster had rounded off preventing shoes from being slackened.

After removing drum (it comes away with wheel and hub bearing after undoing centre nut), the culprit was found to be the lower wheel cylinder. It was freed-off by twisting but really needs replacement.

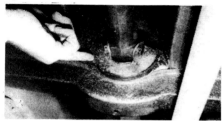

Gearbox rubber mounting at rear of extension has suffered due to the inevitable oil leaks — a candidate for replacement in the future.

At least one rear wheel cylinder has seized too, and handbrake linkage is slack.

Usually you can expect rust trouble in the box sections above the rear axle, but again XLF is in great shape here. New dampers were fitted not long ago, incidentally.
Inner sill walls and jacking points are relatively mud-free and completely sound, so this car at least shouldn't turn into a full-scale rebuild!

Later on we'll be improving the bodywork too, by stripping the paint from some of the suspect areas on the bottoms of the doors and wings, and fitting the repair sections. plus whatever other jobs crop up as our 'new' Ford is pressed into active service. We look forward to an interesting association with this popular little car. ☐

PRACTICAL CLASSICS **ROLLING REBUILD**

Iwas beginning to worry that our latest project car, the 1959 Ford Prefect, was a bit 'too good' for *Practical Classics'* purposes – it has been going just a little too well. We knew from the start that the brakes needed attention and that was given priority (details in next month's *Practical Classics*). As soon as the car was made safe to use, it was pressed into service, first as a back-up staff car and then as a delivery vehicle when our modern van broke down and spares proved hard to find!

With this sort of fairly hard daily use, the faults began to show. The car had been over-heating and there were signs that this was a recurring problem. Traces of jointing compound indicated that the top end of the engine had received attention quite recently and we suspected that the fault would be outside of the engine.

On the sidevalve Ford, the top hose is located at the centre of the head and we started there. We removed the flange at the engine end of the hose to check the thermostat. It definitely wasn't that at fault, someone else had the same idea in the past and had taken the thermostat out. Most cars will run quite satisfactorily without a thermostat – particularly during a summer like 1983 — but the engine will not reach its correct running temperature during the winter.

Ford 100E

Work on our 'rolling rebuild' begins. Geoff L. Prevost details some of the progress we have made on our 1959 Prefect.

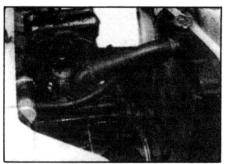

Water in the engine oil could indicate a blown head gasket, one source of overheating. There were signs that top end work had been carried out and that, in this respect, our car was all right. The radiator came out without any problems.

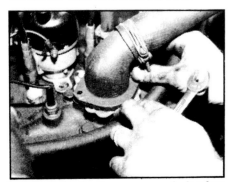

The thermostat housing was removed – but there was no thermostat, ruling that out as a potential cause of the overheating.

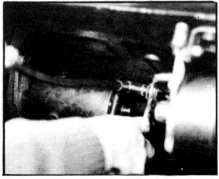

At the starter motor, the HT cable had to be unbolted and removed, it was stretched so tightly . . .

So we moved to the other end of the top hose, to the radiator itself and here, also, a previous owner had been thinking along the same lines – a used radiator was sitting in the boot ready for our local mechanic Ted Landon to fit. Had we not had the spare, we would have tried back flushing the radiator, or using a flushing compound.

...that it had to be removed from the starter solenoid before it would slip off the terminal on the starter motor.

Removing the radiator is simplicity itself. The system needs to be drained by opening the radiator tap (remembering to save the coolant if it contains antifreeze) and detaching the top and bottom hoses. The radiator itself is held in place by four bolts – remove these and lift the radiator out. When reassembling the system, don't forget to close the

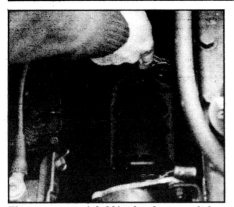

The starter motor is held in place by two set bolts.

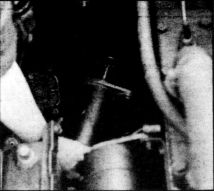

The motor should be pulled forward from the bell housing.

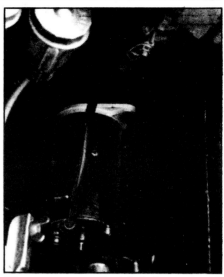

The new starter was fitted the 'other way round' so that the HT cable was not stretched so tightly between the terminals.

The bolts should be loosened evenly and the motor supported. This requires three hands.

drain tap and do remember to top up with antifreeze.

The car went straight back to work after this operation and the overheating problem is no more. Of course, it could just be that the brakes were binding – a not-too-obvious cause of overheating – and as the brakes were sorted out at the same time we will never know for sure.

A few days later, while acting as a van, the Ford refused to start. The starter motor was obviously the culprit and an inexpensive replacement was found locally. Paul Sanderson decided that he would do the motor swop and did so very quickly (see picture sequence). However, when the starter was called upon to act, it whirred uselessly. Ted Landon just *happened* to be passing and he diagnosed a faulty replacement unit!

We were able to get another replacement and even then, the entire job took less than a couple of hours. Yet again the car was pressed back into service and, by the time our 'proper' van was back on the road, Colin, our driver, reported that the 100E was getting 'noisy'.

I drove the car just a few days before this issue went to press and found that the engine is indeed noisy. It begins to knock violently when the revs reach about 2,000 but not necessarily with the engine under load. I suspect the big ends and, with the car now off the road, we will be investigating.

So far, with this running restoration, all of the work has been very simple and could easily have been carried out over a weekend by the least skilled restorer. The car now seems to be presenting some more interesting and involved defects. We will be consulting the spares secretaries of the Ford Sidevalve Owners Club and then preparing our shopping list.

NEXT MONTH
Attending to the brakes and a spring clean!

"Yes, it's the horrible old man from number 38 – we thought we should try and include him in the social life of the Avenue – especially after Malcolm heard about the Anglia he's got locked away in his shed..."

PRACTICAL CLASSICS ROLLING REBUILD

I only drove the 100E once before the brakes were fixed — and that was enough! The only time the brakes worked properly was as the car moved off from standing still when it felt as if it was towing a truck. When it came to slowing the car, the brake pedal felt like a concrete block and stamping very hard on it meant that the 100E would coast to a halt in its own time. All classic symptoms of slave cylinders which were seizing on and off — particularly the unit on one rear wheel which, when it wasn't being driven, would lock up on a loose or wet surface; very disconcerting!

I took the car around to Ted Landon to have the work carried out. We started at the front where we jacked the car up, put it on axle stands and removed the hub caps. Taking off the centre dust cap reveals a castellated nut holding the drum. The split pin should be taken out and that nut, washer and outer bearing removed. Backing the brake shoes right off by turning the adjuster on the backplate anti-clockwise should leave the

Ford 100E

Geoff Le Prevost reports on the progress made with our running restoration.

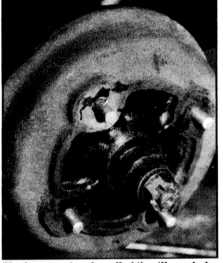

The drums can be taken off while still attached to the road wheel, or they can be removed separately.

The front brakes 'as found'. The washers holding the shoe retaining springs (arowed) must be removed before the shoes can be taken out.

drum free to pull off while still attached to the road wheel.

If the drum proves obstinate, screw the nut, castellated end in, back on to the stub axle (or rear drive shaft) presenting a smooth surface for a hub puller and protecting the threaded end of the shaft from damage.

In spite of the brake binding problems, the drums on all our wheels slipped off quite easily. There are two different front brake layouts. Our 1959 car utilises the later 8 inch drums while pre-1955 cars will have 7 inch drums. There was another change in mid-1955 when adjustable steady posts were found on the front brakes only and later models disposed of them altogether — the shoes rest on three contact points on the backplate. Parts are not necessarily interchangeable, but early models may have been converted to late specification 8 inch drums.

Removing the brake shoes on early models is simply a case of pulling each of the shoes away from the wheel cylinder and removing the spring. Try not to let the shoe slip as, flying back under the force of the spring, it could damage the slave cylinder. Later cars have shoes with springs held by retaining washers which have to be turned through 90 degrees to remove them.

Adjusting the brakes had earlier proved awkward and when the shoes were removed, Ted's suspicions that the snail cam adjusters had worn proved to be well founded. These are 'permanant' fittings and have to be removed with a hammer and chisel. Replacements are held together by a more civilised nut and screw-thread arrangement.

If the slave cylinders are in fair condition, a simple overhaul using a kit of replacement rubber parts may be all that is required. To strip the wheel cylinder, remove the rubber 'boot' and pull out the piston, the seal, the spring seat and the return spring. This can be done with the cylinder in place, but they are easy to remove and this facilitates flushing through. The wheel cylinders are held on either by two small nuts or two setscrews. You should disconnect the pipe which connects the two cylinders on later cars. Now is a good time to check the state of the brake hoses and replace if they show signs of cracking, scuffing or general deterioration.

You should use only clean brake fluid to flush the cylinder through and to lubricate new parts. The pistons in our cylinders were well and truly stuck and had to be forcibly removed with a pair of grips. Even though the barrel and the piston were free of score

The snail cam brake adjusters (arrowed) will almost certainly be worn and should be replaced.

The old adjusters will have to be taken off by force (top) while replacement adjusters fit with the aid of a nut and screw thread.

Hydraulic fluid loss can be kept to a miniumum if brake pipe clamps are used. Check that the pipes are in good condition and check them again when you take the clamp off.

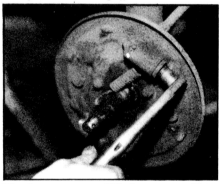

The pistons were very difficult to move and brute force had to be applied to this one — no wonder the brakes didn't work!

The brakes have only one cylinder (expansion housing) which can be seen at the lower end of the brake unit. The device diagonally opposite is the wedge adjuster.

marks, we found that the repair kit was ineffective and we resorted to new cylinders all round.

The rear brakes differ in that there is only one wheel cylinder. This acts on one shoe, pushing it against the drum and then the pressure moves the cylinder body back in its mountings to push the second shoe onto the drum. It sounds complicated, but it is fairly obvious when you see it in front of you. The cylinder (or expander housing) is held in a slot in the backplate with one (or, in later models, two) horseshoe-shaped retaining springs. Again, the drums are 7 inch or 8 inch on later cars.

Whether cylinders have been replaced or overhauled, it is always a good idea to check the bleed nipple before re-assembly. It would be extremely annoying to overhaul a unit, replace it and then have the bleed nipple seize and shear off.

When re-assembling front or rear cylinders, check the seals closely — even new ones care, as particles of dirt may score the piston or short lived. Put the unit back together with care, particles of dirt may score the piston or damage the seals. Grease and oil (other than hydraulic fluid) should also be kept well away from these parts. Put front cylinders together by placing the return spring onto the spring seat and putting them into the cylinder (spring first). Lubricate the seal with brake fluid and carefully push it lipped side first into the cylinder and over the spring seat. Finally, refit the boot.

There is no spring inside the rear wheel cylinders and this unit is put together by inserting the piston seal and then the piston. Late models use a boot retainer clip, but early boots were simply a press fit. When replacing the cylinder, smear a lubricant such as Copaslip on the backplate where the cylinder

will move. Reconnect the brake pipe and handbrake link.

Replace the brake shoes using the reverse of the dismantling order. Again, a dab of Copaslip on the raised contact points will help smooth the brake operation. On back brake shoes and 7 inch front shoes, the leading edge is the one with the greater gap between the end of the shoe and the lining. On 8 inch fronts, it is the end with the tapering web.

Refit the brake drum, washer and outer bearing (front only) then tighten the castellated shaft nut and, of course, fit a new split-pin. Adjust the front brakes by slackening off one snail cam adjuster to bring one shoe well back from the drum, then tighten the other adjuster to lock the drum. Carefully slacken

Brake pipes should be removed by undoing the nut at the rear of the wheel cylinder. Pipes can perish just as much as flexible hoses so check them for corrosion.

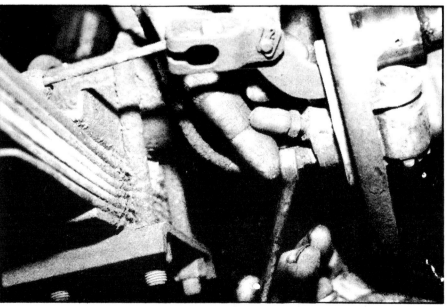

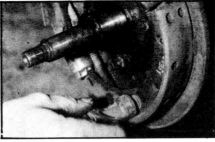

The shoe retaining springs can be removed and replaced using this tool from Girling.

Some work was required on the contact surface of the brake drum. There was evidence that the car had been standing for some time and that the poor brakes had not been making good contact with the drum. The surface was carefully cleaned with emery cloth. There were no signs of distortion.

Refitting the handbrake linkage. The single snail cam adjuster can also be seen.

back this shoe until the wheel is just free to turn then perform the same exercise with the other shoe.

The rear brakes have only one adjuster on the early models. Tighten this until the wheel locks, then slacken off until the wheel is just free, as above. On later models, the leading shoe also has a snail cam adjuster. In this case, lock the wheel by tightening the square-headed wedge adjuster (threaded) then gently tighten the snail cam adjuster (square headed but plain) until you feel the cam just touch the shoe then back the wedge adjuster

off a couple of 'clicks'. When you have adjusted all brakes, check again that the wheels spin freely with no evidence of binding.

The brakes now need bleeding. The bleed valves should have a rubber cup on them but, if this is missing, make sure the nipple and surrounding area is free of dirt. Sometimes, after bleeding, the pedal may still feel

Brake overhaul kits can be obtained for wheel cylinders, but sometimes, as with our car, the cylinder is beyond redemption and must be replaced.

spongy. Check that the front brakes are all adjusted equally, if one is slightly 'out' it could produce the same feel as air in the system.

The handbrake should be checked. If it takes more than four or five 'clicks' to lock the back wheels, then adjust it where the handbrake rod meets the handbrake cables.

The brakes on our 100E are now capable of stopping the car when required but I have now noticed an ominous thump in the rear suspension and I suspect that we might need some new bushes.

Sorting Out Struts

Joss Joselyn Does The MacPherson Strut . . .

It was Michael Brisby, your favourite editor, who said that the MacPherson strut was a Scottish country dance — I think he was joking! Less interestingly, but more accurately, it is a combined suspension and shock absorber unit which also functions as the main steering pivot.

Ford used it as far back as the old 100E and Mk I Consul and it continued from there right through the 105E Anglia and into the Escort and through all the Consuls into the Capri, Corsair and Cortina, both Mk I and Mk II, before it was dropped on the Mk III for an upper and lower wishbone system.

Hillman used it in the Hunter range and the Avenger, and so did quite a lot of other manufacturers. Knowing how to get them out and put them back could be useful to quite a number of car owners.

To find out how to do the job properly, we went up to see Girling in West Bromwich, the people who market inserts designed to replace all the inside of one of these struts.

Before you even think of starting on this job, we must warn you that, if you don't tackle it properly, it can be very dangerous indeed. The big coil spring at the top of the unit is fitted under heavy compression and if it is released without clamping it first, it could take your head off — literally!

So the first thing you do is look at the separate panel over the page and equip yourself with some sort of spring clamp or compressor. Don't think that any old piece of wire will do; it won't! You must have a strong and properly designed device to hold that spring or you will be in trouble.

You will see from the photographs that we used a pair of threaded spring compressors and how there are employed will emerge as you read through the article.

There is an alternative, however — the three heavy steel clamps shown in the photograph. The method of using these is to compress and clamp up the spring before removing the strut.

First, find a couple of heavy people — 12-stoners should be fine and get them to sit on the wing above the strut you are going to work on. Then fit the clamps at three points around the spring, taking in as many of the coils as you can. Once they are in position, wrap a leather belt around or bind them in place with cord. The idea is a 'belt and braces' precaution to make sure the clamps cannot come off the spring and once in place, your heavy friends can go on their way.

Incidentally, there are a few other special tools that might come in very useful, although it is usually possible to manage without them. They are a tool for turning the gland screw at the top of the housing and another tool for cleaning up the threads.

If you are thinking about trying to get hold of these tools, that pre-supposes that you intend dismantling the strut and this would indicate that the damping is not up to the mark and something has to be done about it.

You have two choices — first, you can dismantle the strut and replace the existing piston and valve mechanism by a special Girling insert. This is what we did. The

Sorting Out Struts

(Continued)

alternative is to take the top bearing and spring off the strut and then replace the whole thing with either a new unit or a reconditioned one.

Be very careful if you adopt this latter course that you fit only a manufacturer's reconditioned unit. There have been some very dodgy rebuilds around in the past with old time-expired parts re-used, wrong parts fitted and work dangerously bodged. Unless you do get a recon. strut straight from the manufacturer's agent, use an insert.

Now the strut removal job can start and you can pick up the first step in our photographs and captions.

Talking about Tools

The one tool you must have is some form of clamp or compressor for the coil spring at the top of the unit. Pic. A is the Girling spring compressor and this is available along with a gland nut extractor and a thread chaser as a kit. They are all available separately if preferred.

The three hooked clamps (Pic. B) are one version of another tool which is really a simple clamp. Another is available from a Ford main agent as a Ford part, P 5010. Ford also list a gland nut wrench, Ford tool P 5017, and a tool to remove the top nut, Ford tool P 5025.

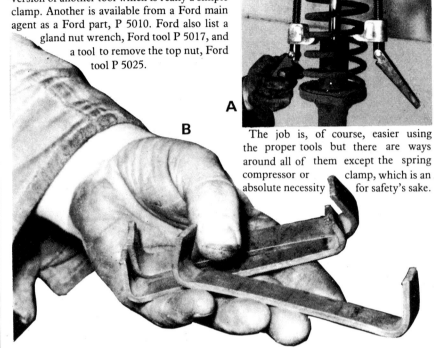

A

B

The job is, of course, easier using the proper tools but there are ways around all of them except the spring compressor or clamp, which is an absolute necessity for safety's sake.

1

Start by lifting the bonnet and loosening off, by just one thread, the large nut at the top of the strut (arrowed) and the three top mounting nuts which can be seen. Do not remove any of them yet.

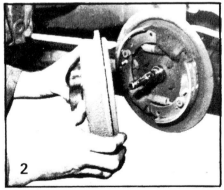

2

Lift the front end of the car and support it on stands positioned at points behind the wheel arches and high enough for the front suspension to hang. Take off the road wheel. Undo the stub axle nut, after removing the split pin and pull off the combined hub bearing/brake drum unit, as shown here.

3

Undo the four nuts and bolts which secure the brake back plate to the foot of the strut.

4

Pull off the brake assembly complete and use a wire loop to support it somewhere convenient so that the flexible hose is neither strained nor kinked.

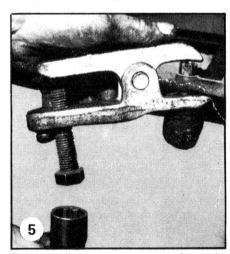

5

It is not strictly necessary to part the steering arm/track rod joint but it does make a tremendous difference to the ease in which you can extract the rear of the three bolts which secure the strut to the lower suspension. Use some sort of joint extractor or if this is not available, a pair of split tapered wedges hammered in. The other method is to impact hammer the joint free. Do this with two hammers, clouting the joint on its sides at two opposite points simultaneously. It is a case of clapping the joint between two hammers until it jars free.

6

Undo and remove the three bottom securing bolts after knocking back the tabs.

7

Disengaging the bottom of the strut is a matter of levering down on the lower half of the suspension and pulling it clear. It takes quite a bit of force to overcome the spring of the anti-roll bar. Once the bottom end is free, the three mounting bolts on top can be fully released and the strut removed from the car. **Do not undo the top centre nut any more than the one turn already made.**

8

Mount the strut in the vice and fit the two spring compressors, taking in as many coils as possible with the clamps fully unwound. Fit them on opposite sides of the spring and then wind them up evenly until the uppermost coil of the spring pulls away from the top plate. It may shift suddenly with quite a crack, so keep your hands well clear of the spring. If you have used the alternative method of compressing the spring beforehand and fitting three clamps, the unit will have come off with this firmly strapped in position and the tension will have already been taken off the spring and the next step can be proceeded with straight away.

9

We undid the top centre nut on both the struts we tackled simply by using a socket and ratchet handle, helped because we started it moving before taking it off the car. Sometimes, however, the whole piston will turn and it will have to be held using an arrangement as shown — a screwdriver or bar in the centre slot to stop it turning. There is another special tool available for this operation but we found we didn't need it.

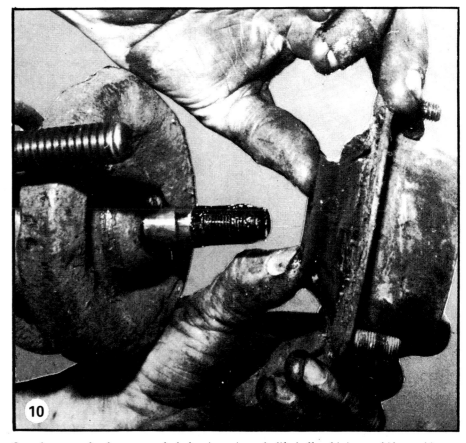

10

Once the top nut has been removed, the bearing unit can be lifted off and it is a good idea at this stage to take the bearings out, wash them in paraffin, pack them with clean HMP grease and refit.

Sorting Out Struts

(Continued)

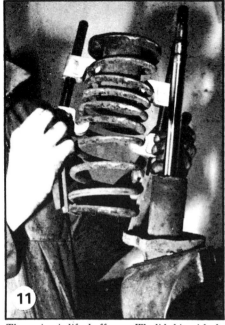

11

The spring is lifted off next. We did this with the two clamps still holding the coils in compression but generally it is recommended that the spring should be released before taking it off and then recompressed for refitting.

Cleaning off the top of the strut will reveal four slots and it is worth cleaning these out thoroughly.

13

Use a suitable punch to knock out the peening in the top of the thread and another punch to tap the gland nut round. If it is reluctant to move, tap the outer housing in the area of the threads to jar them free of possible corrosion.

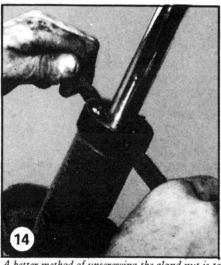

14

A better method of unscrewing the gland nut is to use the Girling special tool. Two pegs on one side are for removing the old gland nut and two on the other side are for screwing in the new one.

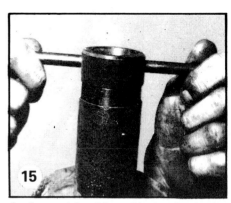

15

Another special tool here, this time for cleaning up the thread. This chaser will clean out any remains of the peening and will also clean up residual thread clogging or damage resulting from a Mazak gland nut which may have been fitted.

16

Like it says on the box, this is the Girling strut repair insert and it replaces the whole of the original innards. What you do is pull out the original piston assembly, tip out the residual oil and just drop the new insert in its place.

Here is the old assembly coming out . . . .

12

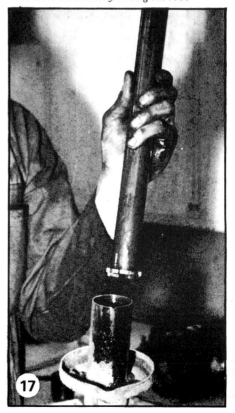

17

18

.... and here is the new one going in.

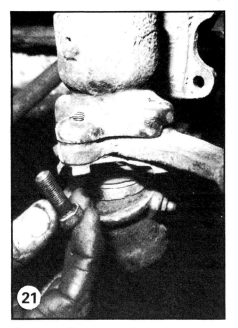

21

One little oddity, when refitting the three bolts, you'll notice that one is longer than the others. It is easy enough to see where it has to go but make sure you get it right. Don't forget the tab washers.

23

Refit the brake backplate assembly. If it looks like ours did when it came off, overhaul it first. We fitted new shoes and wheel cylinders. Then refit the drum and hub bearing assembly. While it is off is a good opportunity to have the bearings out, clean and check them, regrease and refit.

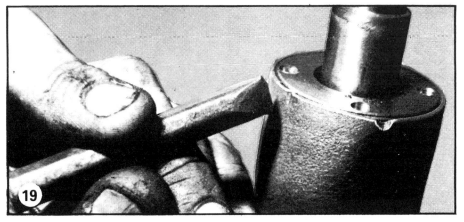

19

After the new gland nut is screwed home, using the Girling tool if you have it, it needs to be peened afresh. The edge of a small cold chisel will do the trick. Screw the gland nut home until it is flush with the top of the tube and take great care not to overtighten it or you might 'bell' the top of the housing. If you can find some way of using a torque wrench with it, 27 lb/ft is the figure you want.

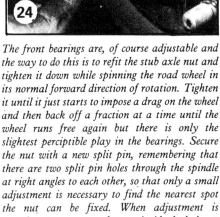

24

The front bearings are, of course adjustable and the way to do this is to refit the stub axle nut and tighten it down while spinning the road wheel in its normal forward direction of rotation. Tighten it until it just starts to impose a drag on the wheel and then back off a fraction at a time until the wheel runs free again but there is only the slightest perciptible play in the bearings. Secure the nut with a new split pin, remembering that there are two split pin holes through the spindle at right angles to each other, so that only a small adjustment is necessary to find the nearest spot the nut can be fixed. When adjustment is complete, put a smear of grease inside the hub cap and refit it and the job is done.

It is seldom that MacPherson struts both fail together and they are not likely to give up. the ghost suddenly either. There are usually warning signs, like fluid leaking, a very lively front end and vague steering or even more spectacular, you may be sitting with the car stopped at lights when one of the front wings bops up in the air! The shocker has locked in the downwards position and then suddenly freed itself again!

If you decide to revitalise your struts, do both of them — it will be like driving a new car. □

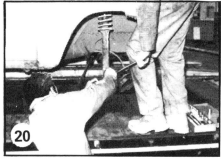

20

The remainder of reassembly is the reverse of dismantling. The spring goes back on, followed by the bearing unit and then the top nut is refitted and tightened down and the maximum figure that can be used is 55 lb/ft. When refitting into the car, use the three nuts to suspend the unit loosely in place and then get help to lever the suspension down and reposition the bottom of the strut.

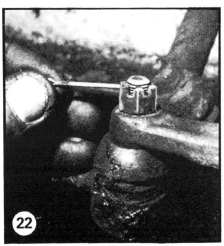

22

Refit the steering arm to the track rod end and tighten the castellated nut down to 20 lb/ft. Lock in place with a new split pin.

Axle Rebuild

Talk to the average DIY man about working on his back axle and he'll look at you as though you said 'brain surgery' or 'nuclear physics'. Even a great many garages shy away from the idea of star and planet wheels, collapsible spacers, pre-load figures and pinion mesh adjustment, but although the action of the differential is difficult to understand, the mechanism of the unit is fairly simple. Probably the biggest mystique of all is in the 'setting up' — the knowhow and special tools that are required.

"Yes, you do need to know what you're doing," says David Hardy of Hardy Engineering, 268 Kingston Road, Leatherhead, Surrey. "Noise and rapid wear are the penalties for getting it wrong, but there aren't as many special tools needed as many people think; nor is the procedure all that complicated. The more adventurous DIY man might well be able to do the job, but the biggest problem is that it is not really financially worthwhile. Usually, it's cheaper to get an exchange unit from a specialist, like us".

When you break down the costs involved, you can quite easily see what he means. A set of bearings cost £30, a crownwheel and pinion, £80, differential gears £30 for the four, plus some other bits and pieces. The axle we show being re-built here is from an Austin Healey Sprite and on exchange it costs £100 from Hardy Engineering. That includes new bearings, new crownwheel and pinion, oilseal and collapsible spacer. Buying just the parts separately would cost around £112, and that doesn't even start to consider the time involved in doing the job yourself or the risk that you might get it wrong. Looking a bit further into costs, an average 1.6 - 2.0-litre saloon works out at about £150; something like a Jaguar would cost up to £350.

It's also worth remembering that there are basically three different types of axle. Proba-

The DIY possibilities might be greater than you think but is a home rebuild financially worthwhile? Joss Joselyn takes a close look in this two-part feature.

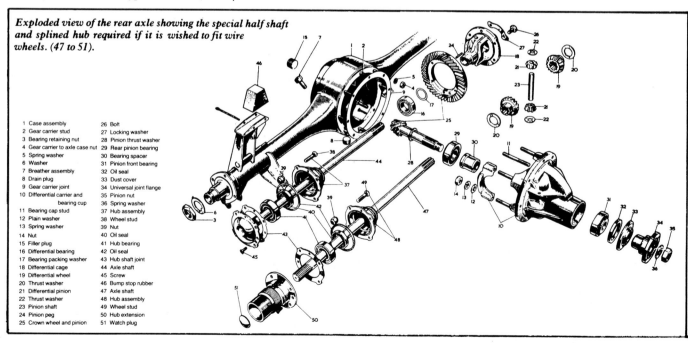

Exploded view of the rear axle showing the special half shaft and splined hub required if it is wished to fit wire wheels. (47 to 51).

1 Case assembly	26 Bolt
2 Gear carrier stud	27 Locking washer
3 Bearing retaining nut	28 Pinion thrust washer
4 Gear carrier to axle case nut	29 Rear pinion bearing
5 Spring washer	30 Bearing spacer
6 Washer	31 Pinion front bearing
7 Breather assembly	32 Oil seal
8 Drain plug	33 Dust cover
9 Gear carrier joint	34 Universal joint flange
10 Differential carrier and	35 Pinion nut
bearing cup	36 Spring washer
11 Bearing cap stud	37 Hub assembly
12 Plain washer	38 Wheel stud
13 Spring washer	39 Nut
14 Nut	40 Oil seal
15 Filler plug	41 Hub bearing
16 Differential bearing	42 Oil seal
17 Bearing packing washer	43 Hub shaft joint
18 Differential cage	44 Axle shaft
19 Differential wheel	45 Screw
20 Thrust washer	46 Bump stop rubber
21 Differential pinion	47 Axle shaft
22 Thrust washer	48 Hub assembly
23 Pinion shaft	49 Wheel stud
24 Pinion peg	50 Hub extension
25 Crown wheel and pinion	51 Watch plug

Use a hammer and punch to mark the bearing caps (two dots on the crownwheel side and one on the other side). Undo the nuts and remove together with one plain and one spring washer on each. Knock the caps off gently using a hammer.

Lever out the differential carrier unit complete. A firm action with two screwdrivers is the best technique.

There is a special tool for holding the pinion flange while unscrewing the pinion nut, but the vice can be used as a substitute. Here a special long angle-iron lever is employed with the appropriate socket. This is necessary because the nut is done up to 140 lb/ft. Clean up any damage to the flange afterwards with a file.

Tap the end of the pinion shaft, and the pinion flange should come free easily. Continue tapping with a hammer and drift to knock the pinion through. With it will come the inner part of the rear bearing. The outer track and the front bearing complete are left behind in the nose piece.

Use a long thin drift via the small cutaway shown to remove the inner part of the front bearing.

A long drift used together with a hammer will drive out the outer tracks for both bearings; the front one this way and the rear one from the other side of the nose piece.

Here is the pinion shaft, together with the collapsible spacer, which is thrown away. A new one will be needed when reassembling. Note there is also another washer under the bearing, which must be retained.

Getting the rear bearing off the shaft is not easy without the special tool shown here. It is clamped in place so that the thin shaped plates of the tool supported the underside of the bearing while the pinion shaft is knocked through it. If a press is available, this is even better.

Knock back the tab washers from the heads of the six high-tensile bolts which secure the crownwheel to its carrier, and remove the bolts.

Rotate the crownwheel and carrier assembly, using a hammer and suitable drift on the rim of the crownwheel to tap it free.

bly the most common is the Salisbury, where the differential is built into the axle casing. There is the independent rear suspension type, which is a totally self-contained unit, with two separate driveshafts. Then there is the banjo unit, where the differential assembly can be lifted out of the axle in a single lump, and that's the one we've tackled here.

In addition to the Sprite, this type is also fitted to the Morris 1000, Healey 3000, Marina, Escort, Capri, Anglia, early Cortina, old MG's, MGA, etc., old Sunbeams, Consuls, Zephyr Zodiac, and the 100E among others. It's not exactly rare!

The most common back axle problem is noise, when that "wanga wanga, wang" sound becomes really obtrusive on drive, or on overrun, or both. The most common reason is pitting in the differential bearings. If the unit runs out of oil at any time, that's much more serious, because then the crownwheel and pinion have to be replaced. A broken tooth is rare and again is the result of running out of oil. The driver is rarely left in any doubt if this has happened.

Getting the unit out rarely provides any great difficulty. I once took one out of an old Zephyr perched precariously on top of a pile

C O N T I N U E D

Axle Rebuild

C O N T I N U E D

You need a long parallel pin punch to knock the locking pin out of the cross shaft in the carrier. The tip as it emerges is arrowed in the photograph.

Now the drift can be used to push out the cross shaft, or gently drift it out if it's a little tight.

Rotate the planet gears inside the carrier until they are adjacent to a window and can be lifted out together with their cup-shaped thrust washers.

Now the two star gears can be removed from the carrier.

Another job that's not too easy without special tools is drawing off the differential bearings. The job is best done in a press but two levers hooked under the edge of the inner race can be used like this.

When the bearing is off, carefully retain the shim pack for each side and do not mix them up.

It only needs very slight marking on the teeth of a differential planet gear to make the unit noisy. Arrowed here is an example of undercutting. See the wear line half way up each tooth, shown by arrows.

Scuffing is what you'll be looking for on the crownwheel and an example is shown here. It's quite enough to make the unit noisy. Broken teeth, incidentally, are rare, except in a unit which has run out of oil.

of other cars in a breaker's yard. It was raining, so it was miserable as well as dicey, but mechanically it was no trouble.

Mainly the work consists to taking off the rear wheels and brake drums, releasing the shaft flanges and pulling the halfshafts outwards, clear of the diff unit. The propshaft is disconnected at the rear flange and dropped clear, then the ring of bolts around the differential nosepiece is undone and the nosepiece lifted out with the rest of the unit attached.

On the bench, the unit can be further dismantled along the lines of our photo-sequence and captions, which is more or less self-explanatory. Much depends on the work you want to do. Obviously, if you just want to fit new bearings, you wouldn't need to dismantle the whole thing. The pinion bearings also wear, however, and that means a lot more dismantling. While the unit is apart, also examine the crownwheel and pinion teeth for scuffing, scoring, or chipping.

If there is any damage, both components will have to be renewed as a pair. Never change just one without the other.

Similarly, wear may be found on the planet and star gears of the differential. This may take the form of the undercutting visible in the photographs; these gears too need renewing as a set.

Immerse all the parts in a bath of cleaning fluid and use an old paintbrush to ensure they are scrupulously clean. Clean up the vice jaws and cover the bench being used so that everything stays clean. Dirt and grit inside the assembly would be catastrophic!

NEXT MONTH
Reassembling the differential unit

Axle Rebuild

Last month we looked closely at the dismantling of the rear axle — in particular the differential — and investigated some of the likely wearing areas.

In this issue, the reassembly of the unit is covered in some detail in the photographs and captions and the only area likely to cause any problems is setting up and adjustment. There are three main checks, and the first of these is the pre-load on the pinion. At Hardy Engineering, with years of experience, they are able to do this by 'feel'. Simply nipping the nut down on the collapsible spacer until it feels right.

The official method is to tighten the nut initially to 140 lb/ft with a torque wrench. Then a spring balance is hooked in the top hole of the pinion flange and pulled in the direction of rotation. The flange should turn at about 8lb. If the figure is higher than this, you'll need a thinner thrust washer; if it is too low, use a thicker one. Each time it is changed, however, you'll have to fit a new spacer. This must never be used twice.

Backlash between the crownwheel and pinion can be measured as described using a dial gauge, and should be around eight thou.

The check on the meshing of the crownwheel and pinion, as explained in the photographs and captions, is done using engineer's blue. Put pressure on the crownwheel and turn the pinion flange until

In the second part of this two-part feature, Joss Joselyn covers the reassembly of the rear axle differential and shows how fine adjustment is achieved.

Make doubly sure you are using the right shim pack and fit it under the new bearing. With any sort of substantial mileage, always fit new bearings.

Driving them down evenly is best ensured by spreading the load across the bearing. Here a cold chisel is used but a block of wood would do as well.

After inspecting the star gears for any signs of undercutting, refit them in the carrier.

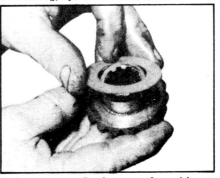

Make sure you fit them together with new washers.

Now the planet gears can go in, once again ensuring they are equipped with new washers.

the crownwheel moves a half turn. This will provide marks on the drive side of the crownwheel teeth. Reversing this process, putting load on the flange and turning the crownwheel anti-clockwise will provide meshing marks on the other (overrun) side of the teeth.

What the marks should be and what you do to correct them are shown in the table. Although the marks in the little 'tooth' diag-

CONTINUED

Axle Rebuild

C O N T I N U E D

Rotate the assembly until the holes in the planet gears and the carrier line up and then push home the cross shaft.

Line up the hole in the cross shaft with the one in the carrier and then insert the locking pin, driving it home firmly with a punch.

Fit the old crownwheel if it is satisfactory, or a new one if it isn't, using six new bolts and new tab washers. Tighten the bolts to 60 lb/ft and make sure you turn up the tabs to lock the bolts.

Refit the thrust washer on the pinion shaft and follow this with the inner part of the bearing.

Invert the assembly, supporting the bearing on the vice jaws, protect the face of the pinion from direct impact (here a cold chisel is used) and hammer the pinion shaft down into the bearing.

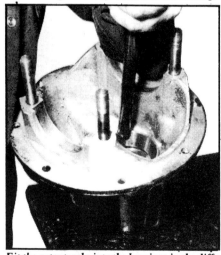

Fit the outer tracks into the housings in the differential nose piece, simply reversing the method used to drive them out. Tap them home evenly and straight, using the drift all round the rim. It's a very good idea to heat the casing first. It will avoid damaging the tracks.

Here's the outer track of the front bearing going in. Note that it is inserted from the other side.

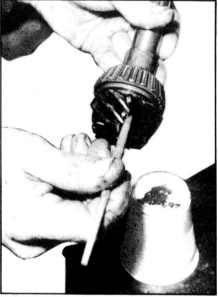

The teeth of pinion are now painted with engineer's blue. Hardy Engineering use Prussian blue oil paint, which is cheaper and does the job just as well. Make sure both sides of all the teeth are covered.

Stand the pinion on a 4in. block, fit the new collapsible spacer, and drop the nose piece over it and ensure it seats properly on the inner bearing.

Drop in the centre part of the front bearing.

Tap round the inner edge evenly to seat it.

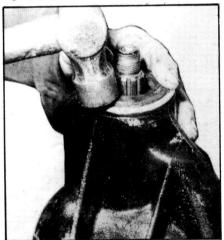

Insert a new oil seal, gently tapping round the edge to seat it evenly and without damage.

Insert the dust cover/pinion flange assembly onto the splines, using a bar across the top of the flange to help drive it down evenly. Follow this with the spring washer and nut and use the socket and a torque wrench to tighten it until it just nips on the bearings.

Tap the pinion shaft from both ends to settle the bearings and then tighten the pinion shaft again if necessary.

As a final check of pre-load, use a small screwdriver to 'feel' the bearing rollers behind the pinion and make sure there is no movement.

Now move the crownwheel backwards and forwards to check backlash between the crownwheel and pinion, which should be approximately 0.008in. (8 thou). Hardy Engineering do this whole thing by 'feel', but it can also be checked using a dial gauge. This is set up on the casing and the measurement made on one of the crownwheel teeth.

Another check is made by putting pressure on the crownwheel and turning the pinion flange in a clockwise direction until the crownwheel has rotated half a turn. This gives marks on the drive side of the teeth which can be inspected. If satisfactory, put the load on the pinion flange and rotate the crownwheel to give the marks on the overrun side. If either of these sets of marks is unsatisfactory, the setting must be altered in accordance with the accompanying table. ▼

TOOTH CONTACT CHART

	Tooth Contact		Condition	Remedy
A	HEEL (outer end) / Coast / Drive / TOE (inner end)		IDEAL TOOTH CONTACT evenly spread over profile, nearer toe than heel.	
B	HEEL (outer end) / Coast / Drive / TOE (inner end)		HIGH TOOTH CONTACT heavy on the top of the drive gear tooth profile.	Move the Drive PINION DEEPER into MESH. i.e. Reduce the pinion cone setting.
C	HEEL (outer end) / Coast / Drive / TOE (inner end)		LOW TOOTH CONTACT heavy in the root of the drive gear tooth profile.	Move the Drive PINION OUT of MESH. i.e. Increase the pinion cone setting.
D	HEEL (outer end) / Coast / Drive / TOE (inner end)		TOE CONTACT hard on the small end of the drive gear tooth.	Move the Drive GEAR OUT of MESH. i.e. Increase backlash.
E	HEEL (outer end) / Coast / Drive / TOE (inner end)		HEEL CONTACT hard on the large end of the driving gear tooth.	Move the Drive GEAR INTO MESH. i.e. Decrease backlash but maintain minimum backlash.

Drop the complete assembly back into the carrier, replace the bearing caps, making sure they are the right way round as indicated by the punch marks before dismantling. Lock them down with plain washers, spring washers and nuts.

rams are 'hatched' lines, they will show as clear metal areas in the blue paint in actual practice.

Whether you do decide to have a go at rebuilding your own diff or not is up to you. If the work is tackled with care, an acceptable result is possible and the penalty for not getting it exactly right may well be nothing more than an axle that's slightly noisy.

One final thought. Whether you tackle the work or get an expert, like Hardy Engineering, to do it, when you refit the unit, just don't forget to refill with the correct grade of oil. □

The writer would like to thank Hardy Engineering, 268 Kingston Road, Leatherhead, Surrey for their assistance in this article.

PRACTICAL CLASSICS ROLLING REBUILD

Our 1959 Ford 100E Prefect was purchased primarily as the first in our rolling rebuild series but – apart from a very short spell as a back-up delivery vehicle – it has spent much more time being rebuilt than it has rolling! During the car's spell of active life, a severe bottom end knocking became evident and was soon diagnosed as big end failure. The car was taken off the road and plans were made to rebuild the bottom end of the engine.

While talking to Steve Waldenberg on a different subject (Steve is the spares co-ordinator of the Ford Sidevalve Owners' Club) I mentioned the plight of our car and he suggested stripping the engine before we decided what to do with it. For a start, the big end bearings could have been either white metal or the more's 'modern' separate shells.

On early cars (built before August 1954) the engine and gearbox have to be taken out in one piece. On our later car, they could be separated and the engine removed while leaving the 'box in situ. This can be achieved by removing an inspection cover to gain access to two of the clutch housing bolts – and this is the only part of the operation which is anything out of the ordinary.

One of the first considerations when removing an engine is space – you need to be able to get at the unit to lift it, and you need somewhere to put it when it is out. First job, then, is to remove the bonnet and then take out the battery. Drain the cooling system (keeping the coolant in a clean container if you wish to save your antifreeze) by opening the drain tap at the bottom of the radiator. The cylinder block does not have a drain tap. Water flow will be greatly increased if you drain the system with the radiator pressure cap removed.

All leads, cables and controls should now be disconnected. This is really only a matter of common sense – just undo everything that would otherwise prevent the engine from leaving home. Undo the exhaust clamp bolts and remove the two halves of the clamp. When you undo the fuel feed pipe, remember to plug it as fuel can syphon down from the tank. The radiator should be removed by releasing the top and bottom hoses and undoing the four retaining bolts. Take off the heater hoses as well.

The rubber tube connected to the manifold powers the windscreen wipers and should be removed. The distributor should be removed from any engine during removal or replacement and on this unit, take note of the distributor index setting, then undo the screw and locking washer holding the distributor to the head. Unclip the HT leads from the spark plugs and lift the distributor away.

The starter motor and the dynamo should

Ford 100E

Geoff Le Prevost discovers a disaster area

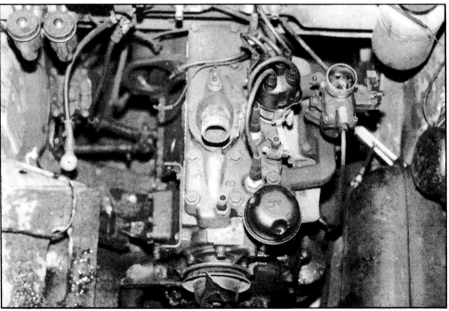

Almost ready to lift. The distributor and the manifolds can be left in place, but we would recommend that you remove them before the lifting starts.

be removed and taking off the fan blades will give a bit more room to work in. Work can now begin on releasing the engine itself. Release the single nut on the engine mount-

ings then move inside the car. Remove the larger inspection cover by undoing the self-tapping screws and then release the two upper clutch housing bolts which are in the

The 100E engine is heavier than you might think, so make sure your lifting gear is up to the job.

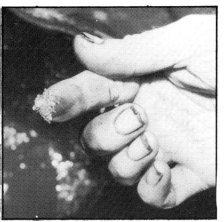

The evidence. Particles of what was a big end bearing form the greater part of the sludge found at the bottom of the sump. Bad news for our 100E engine.

The slivers of metal are also found on the strainer gauze of the oil pick-up pipe. Smaller particles will almost certainly have found their way through and will have caused further havoc in other bearings around the engine.

forward and upper part of the recess around the gear lever. Under the car now to release the remaining flywheel housing to clutch bolts, having first supported the gearbox with a jack or other suitable solid object.

The 100E engine, in spite of its compact size, is a heavy lump of iron and you will need fairly substantial lifting gear to move it around. Never get into the position when you have to to work with any part of your anatomy underneath a suspended engine. You only have to see the damage a tumbling engine can do to a concrete floor to imagine the harm it could do to your foot.

To lighten the engine very slightly, you could drain the engine oil and this is really the last stage at which you can safely do this. To remove the engine, fit a lifting sling and attach it to the hoist. Lift the engine slightly then pull it forward to clear the main gearbox drive. It is easier to push the car backwards with the engine hoisted high enough to clear the front bulkhead than it is to maneouvre the engine forwards on the lifting gear (which is very dangerous).

With our engine safely on the floor, we were able to remove the sump by releasing the fourteen bolts and locking washers. The appalling state of affairs was all too obvious from the evidence shining in the sump sludge. The white metal bearings were not just worn, they had disintegrated! The tens of thousands of tiny fragments littered the engine and were also to be found adhering to the filter gauze on the oil pump assembly. We lifted a bearing cap just to prove that the damage was extensive. It was a disaster area!

Mechanic Ted Landon, who has been carrying out most of the work on this car, considered that the rebuild on this particular engine would be very expensive. The oil could well have carried the debris to every moving part and we agreed that the only logical course of action would be to look for a replacement.

By one of those strange quirks of fate, we heard from a reader who just happened to have a 100E engine which he offered to sell to us. We will be looking into the offer and hope to be able to report some success next month.

There are times in a rebuild when it no longer makes economical sense to continue with that you have and you have to look around for something better to work with. In the case of engines, there are still a great number of units from 'our' period lying around, if not in scrapyards any more, then at least in lockups and workshops around the country. If you cannot find what you are looking for in classified advertisements, then it often pays to place a 'want' ad detailing your requirements.

The white metal bearing which had been bonded to the con rod (lower section) shows sign of advanced decay and disintegration.

PRACTICAL CLASSICS **ROLLING REBUILD**

When managing editor Paul Skilleter first saw the 100E which was to become our first rolling rebuild project car, he was impressed with the basic soundness of the vehicle's body. Apart from a little surface rust beneath each bumper blade, the only serious corrosion was at the rear of the sills and the bottom of the front wings just behind the front wheels. We wondered what we would find 'below the surface' when we started to remove panels – and we were delighted to discover that Paul's analysis had been correct, it is indeed a very sound car.

We bought a couple of sills and two front wing repair panels from 100E specialist Steve Waldenberg, of Roundhay Motors, 71 Commercial Road, Leeds and took them down to Malcolm Grey Engineering at West Malling, Kent. A quick inspection of the underside proved that we need have no fears there.

There are two ways to fit sills to this type of car. One is the quick way where the old sill is cut out leaving 'plates' under each door post, then making identical cut outs from the new sill and welding it around the door panels, and there is the 'proper' way, where every scrap of the old sill is removed and the new one is fitted exactly as original.

A garage carrying out a similar repair to a modern car might well follow the quick method, but we elected to do the job in full. We wanted to make sure our car was as original, that it had as much strength built in as it did when it was new, and, not least, we wanted scope to manipulate the pattern sills into the best possible fit.

It is quite wrong to repair a sill which has a structural function — welding or rivetting on repairs should not be done. Fitting a sill over an existing sill is also wrong. Fitting a part sill is marginally acceptable if carried out by an expert who is repairing accident rather than rust damage — generally the box created by the sill is a vital stiffening member; part repairs might well articulate that box. Try very hard to obtain a factory sill and avoid galvanised sills, they are hard to weld.

The first task is to make sure that the new panels are indeed what you ordered. You would look very silly having hacked off the sill on the driver's side only to find that a busy order office has sent you two passenger side sills. Offer the panel up to the still-intact body to check that the contours are right for that particular model.

Work on one side of the car only and use the other side for reference when something doesn't make sense. Before starting work, position the car so that the doors on the side being worked on can be opened fully. The workshop floor should be solid to support a jack and level to reduce the risk of the car being twisted. All inflammable materials in

Ford 100E

Geoff Le Prevost reports on repair panels for our Prefect

the garage and in the vicinity of the repair (interior trim etc) should be removed. You should also have a fire extinguisher handy.

We elected to remove the doors to improve access and to relieve strain on the door pillars which would later be unsupported at the bottom. The doors should be checked for hinge wear before removing, and hinge positions should be scribed to ease refitting — make a note of the positions of any packing pieces or washers.

Replacing the bottom edge of the front wing is a job which goes very much hand in hand with replacing the sills on the 100E. If you aren't repairing the wing, it has to come off because the sill is rebated behind it. The repair panel 'cut out' should therefore be made first.

The panel should be offered up into position and the top diagonal line marked on the wing. If you intend to butt weld the joint, make your cut on this line but, if you are going to set the edge of the wing back to make a lap joint, you should scribe a cutting line about half to one inch on the 'waste' side of

the original line. The section can then be removed using a cutting tool. Malcolm used a cutting wheel on an angle grinder.

When offering the panel up, Malcolm noted that there was no provision to fold metal over on the curve beside the front door. To compensate, Malcolm used a grinding disc to grind away the existing fold so that he could remove the section, but still leave a free 'lip' of metal to act as a rough pattern and provide a double skinned edge to the wing when welded to the edge of the repair panel.

Removing the lower section of the wing reveals the lower wing mounting bolt thread and provides an opportunity to dose the threads with a freeing agent to ease removal. The bolt head can be reached from under the wing. The lower section of the inner wing, although not badly corroded, was removed and a pattern section was made and later fitted. Removal of this part made getting to the front of the sill a little bit easier.

The sills were removed using an air chisel to cut some awkward areas. We appreciate that this is a tool not readily available so we also used a hammer and cold chisel and then an angle grinder — tools which should be available to the home restorer. Be careful that sparks from the angle grinder do not strike the car's glass or paintwork, the marks cannot be removed. Also, be on the lookout for wiring looms which are occasionally fed through car sills. When doing any cutting or grinding work, it is wise to wear protective gloves and goggles are essential.

On many cars, the sills will fall off with very little encouragement, but these proved a little more recalcitrant. Malcolm chiselled the sills out leaving an inch or so still attached to the car. These strips were removed by

To replace the sills, the front wing must either be removed or cut to fit a repair panel. The panel should be offered up and an initial guide line scribed on the wing. The cutting line is then scribed a short distance below.

The wing seam was released using an angle grinder...

...leaving a strip to weld the new panel on to, so giving double thickness at the door aperture.

The old sills were removed using a variety of cutting tools. Here, the air chisel is brought into play to remove the bulk of the sill.

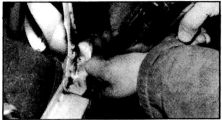

Saw cuts were made through the top plates to the inner sills...

... Spot welds were then released by grinding them with an angle grinder.

The angle grinder was again brought into play to remove the bottom seam.

Spot welds at the base of the front door pillar were drilled out.

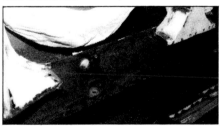

The clean and surprisingly sound inner sill needed little work.

releasing the spot weld either by drilling or by cutting into them with a grinder (which proved quicker and easier than drilling, provided there was space to use the angle grinder).

Removal of the outer sills revealed surprisingly intact inner sills apart from an area at the rear beneath the rust patch on the outer sill. This was cut out and a simple, square repair section let in. There had to be *some* rot so in a way we were relieved to find this and

The central pillar was also released in order to slot the new sill behind it. It is a good idea to mark the inner sill so that rewelding the pillar can be done accurately.

An aperture for the jacking point must be cut into the new sill.

a small area of frayed wheel arch – the part which acts as the rear closing plate to the sill.

The main 'body' of the sills came off quite easily, it was removing the 'remains' which was the difficult part. Taking these pieces off involves any types of cutting tool which fits the job, remembering that you cannot be as brutal with the metal which has to remain on the car as you could be with the scrap parts of the sill.

Some care needs to be taken with the metal which forms the bottom edge of the door pillars although small holes can be filled with weld and distortion which hasn't travelled too far up the pillar can be dressed out with a hammer and dolly. When every last scrap has been removed, the mating areas need to be ground down to clean metal so that they will accept weld.

At this point, the new sill can be offered up to check for fit. Ours needed to be trimmed slightly to fit behind the front door pillar and a small square had to be cut to clear the jacking point. Our sills appeared to be just a fraction too long which meant we had to modify the rear end slightly by cutting down the top flange, then cutting, shortening and rewelding the back edge of the panel.

Most of the time taken in fitting any panel is used up making the final adjustments. Take time offering the sill up, clamping it in position, then standing back to see where it fits and where it doesn't as well as whether

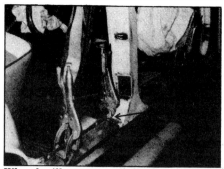

When the sill was eventually lined up to Malcolm Gray's satisfaction, it was clamped then pop rivetted. The centre pillar was drilled and bolted (at the point arrowed) to the sill and inner sill to support the doors which were hung for checking the sill shape and door gaps.

With the doors on, it was easy to see that the sill shape was not quite right. This was corrected as far as possibly be careful application of pressure from a bottle jack. A small rust hole can be seen in the curved panel above the sill – and it can also been seen that the sill is a little long.

the adjustments you are going to make will affect other areas of fit. This is time well spent if you want the car to be the right shape and if you want the doors to open and close.

When the outer sill matches up the inner sill and all the door posts sit comfortably over the sill, replace the doors to check the bottom gap. While the doors were on, the centre pillar was drilled and temporarily bolted to the sills. When the doors were fitted, Malcolm found some distortion proving that while the inner flanges might mate up perfectly, this doesn't mean that the rest of the panel is the

right shape. The profile was corrected very carefully using a combination of bottle jacks and load spreading pieces of wood and an occasional persuasive bit of man handling.

When the fit was as good as it could be, the sill was rivetted to hold it in place while the first few welds were made. You could also use self tapping screws. This is another good time to check that there is nothing in the immediate area which might suffer from the heat of welding — trim for instance.

In our case, Malcolm elected to use a variety of welding techniques to secure the 100E sills. The top and bottom flanges were spot welded and the bottom edges of the pillars were plug welded using a gas torch and the holes made when removing the old spot welds. This produced a finish very close to the original but without sophisticated spot welder arms.

If you do not have a spot welder, the top and bottom flanges can be seam welded or you could drill the new sill and plug weld. A small amount of brazing was used on the D-post to restore a curve which was lost during the repair.

The front wing repair section was then fitted. Malcolm used an edge setting tool to provide a locating lip on the existing wing edge and then spot welded the repair section to this. It is almost as easy to lap weld this panel using a gas torch. The 'fold' at the door

aperture was restored by seam welding the new panel to the strip of steel left by grinding off the old wing. The gap was filled with lead solder – if you used a gas welder, the line of weld can be dressed down using a grinder. □

PRACTICAL CLASSICS **ROLLING REBUILD**

We might have mentioned before that the greatest part of the work involved in respraying the car comes *before* the paint is mixed, but I think it bears repetition. Some people have the mistaken impression that a fresh lick of paint will cover all the blemishes and faults on a car body, or at least, hide them. In fact, paint has a curious ability to highlight every scratch, dent or stonechip. After a respray, every scuff, ripple or ill-fitting panel will be thrown into stark relief if the work hasn't been done. If you haven't got a perfect base to work on, there is no way you will get a perfect paint finish.

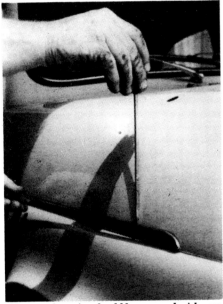

Chrome trim strips should be removed with care. Small scratches from the screwdriver blade can be flatted down but wrap the blade in a rag if you do not intend to respray that area.

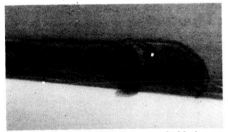

The trim clips were dirty but remarkably intact. This is usually one of the first areas to rot – yet another indication of how sound this car is.

During the past few months, while carrying out restoration work on our Ford 100E Prefect, we have been impressed by the generally good state of the car. However, when it comes to the body work, it quickly became apparent that a 'while-u-wait' respray just would not be good enough. Had we not

Ford 100E

Our Prefect goes to paint, and Geoff Le Prevost reports on the problems.

replaced body panels (we had to fit new sills) we would not have repainted the car, the original paint, although getting old, would have sufficed.

After some debate – and one false start – we decided to have the whole car resprayed in its original Conway Yellow. While we were not looking for a concours finish, we wanted the car to look presentable as we will be holding on to it for a while and taking it to a number of meetings and rallies. We asked Malcolm Gray, who replaced the sills for us, if he would tackle the paint as well.

It became obvious on examination that the body of the car bore all of the hallmarks of age without the usual signs of severe corrosion. There was surface rust on the front apron and rear skirt but when this was sanded down, clean metal shone through. No, the problem wasn't rust, it was all those little 'parking bruises' and nicks in the old paintwork.

To begin with, all of the brightwork was taken off the car, the side strips being gently levered off. They are all fitted on to 'button' clips with none of the little bolts at the rear

end which some cars have and which you only discover when the chrome strip has been bent to a right angle! The buttons seem similar to those used on the MGB. Those which have not deteriorated can be carefully drilled out and saved for re-use with fresh pop rivets. The grime underneath can be washed off or, if stains are persistant, a de-greaser will remove the worst and the flatting down process will do the rest.

The bumpers, radiator grille, wing mirrors, door and boot handles, headlamp sur-

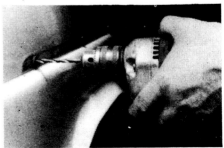

The rivets securing the clips were drilled out and the 'buttons' saved for re-use.

rounds, rear light assemblies and sun visor were all removed with little difficulty. If you find that nuts or bolts are rusted tight, be very careful about splashing lubricants around. Many of the spray lubricants contain silicon, and silicon (particularly the modern polishes) are death to re-sprays. Once the stuff is on the car, you'll never get rid of it and you don't know you've got it until the final colour coats go on, then the surface breaks down into fish eye craters and you have to start again.

Surface rust on the front apron was sanded down to bare metal.

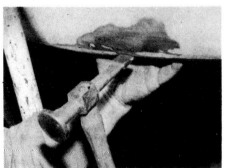

Small dents and irregularities were straightened out with a hammer and dolly.

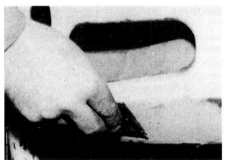

The surface imperfections were smoothed using a quick setting stopper.

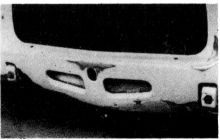

The front of the car was given a final flatting down before etching primer was applied (see heading picture).

The editor refused to be photographed wearing rubber gloves, but this would be a wise precaution when using paint stripper such as Nitromors.

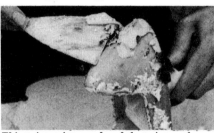

This paint stripper reduced the paint on the rear light assemblies to jelly within twenty minutes.

The name badges are held on with a combination of spring clips, which you have to lever off from behind the panel, and captive clips (usually when the fitting is sited over a box section) which means that you have to lever the badge away from the front. Both are nerve racking as you can terminally damage the studs, the clips or even the badge itself.

The areas of surface rust were taken back to bare metal and the paint edges featherd to give a smooth contour. Stone chips and scratches were stopped while dents and distortions were beaten out and then stopped to give a smooth surface. The areas of bare steel were sprayed with etching primer – this is quite important as it gives the fresh coat of paint something to 'grip'.

One of the things which had been noted about this particular car was the appalling fit

The underside of the sun visor had a fine covering of rust but this was rubbed down and resprayed in its original grey.

The remaining paint flecks were removed with a wire brush and then the light units were lightly rubbed over with hand-held emery cloth, etch primed and sprayed off the car.

of all four doors, so we asked Malcolm to take a stab at squaring them off. The doors were all re-hung with the appropriate packing washers added where necessary but the overall result was really not to his satisfaction. The truth seems to be that the doors do not fit the apertures and probably never did – back in the fifties, production line tolerances were not everything they could have been.

With all of the bare metal and repair areas etch-primed and the driver's door totally primed, it was time for the first colour coat. This was due to go on just as we were sending this issue to press, a week before the Bromley Pageant – when the car was due to make its public debut. More news of our Project will follow soon when Paul Skilleter puts this car to work. ☐

Preparing your car for winter involves a lot more than just squirting a bit of Waxoyl into the sills — it should really be looked on as a sort of full 'autumn service', so that every part of the car is protected against the elements, not simply the body shell. There is a lot to do as well, so reserve at least two and preferably three or four complete weekends if you want to carry out the job properly!

I will assume first of all that we are talking about a 'working' car, one that is going to be used almost every day (later on we will examine what is involved in 'laying up' a vehicle), and a good starting point is the exterior. If you recall last month's instalment, you will remember that it is water that allows the electro-chemical rust action to take place, so the underlying aim must always be to exclude it.

To do this, arm yourself with a water repellant like WD40, or one of the cavity-protectors like Supertrol or Comma's Wax Seal in an oil can, and get the stuff into all painted body seams, behind bumpers, and wherever the shell is pierced by accessories like mirrors or chrome strips. Wipe off the excess with a rag dampened with turps, then polish. As an alternative to constantly cleaning the brightware, you can give the chrome itself a light coating too, repeating it every few weeks — you can wipe it off next spring when the salt stops, and it is about the only way you can prevent those ugly red specks from appearing on your bumpers . . .

This is a good time to rub down and re-touch all those stone chips, which otherwise

WINTER PROTECTION

Protect behind chrome, and along seams like the one below headlight, with a water-dispersant. Treating the chrome itself will go a long way to preserving it too.

will blister merrily away; those new glass-fibre abrasive pencils are ideal for this job, and when you have got the worst of the rust out, you can use a rust-killer or primer to kill any left before applying the touch-in paint. The main point to watch here is to ensure you don't leave any rust around the circumference of the chip, the most common cause of touch-in repairs failing after a few months. Also, make this the time to tackle any leaks — Seak 'n Seal is good under windscreen rubbers, though it never quite dries out and if

Paul Skilleter examines the methods you can use to preserve your classic during the wet winter months.

you leave excess on the outside it tends to collect dirt.

Next, open all the doors and go round with a piece of wire clearing out the drain holes — it is amazing how easily they become blocked, thanks to many manufacturers being very mean with the size of them. Ineffective drain holes is the major reason why doors rot — the water lies in the bottom keeping the metal constantly wet. Check all other drain holes too — there are a surprising number on most cars, in the sills, under bulkhead sides, where inner and outer wings meet on the underside, and in chassis sections. If your car has a sun roof, clear out its drainage points too. Do not hesitate to enlarge measly ones or drill any number of additional drain holes — water

will get away that much quicker and even if you were not to use anti-rust fluid afterwards, you would add usefully to the lifespan of your car.

Now we come to treating the enclosed sections of the bodyshell; this is largely a matter of getting a wax or oil-based substance inside all cavities, using whatever tools you have or are supplied with in the rust-proofing kits. Here, the amateur is at a disadvantage to the professional rust-proofer, who has a range of special spray heads and probes to get the material where it is most needed, using compressed air or high-pressure pumps. But what you lack in equipment you can largely make up for using patience and dedication – plus the fairly liberal use of whatever anti-

WINTER PROTECTION/Continued

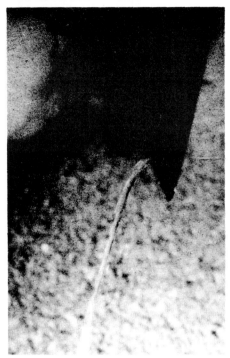

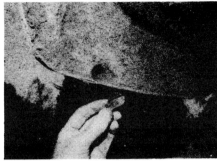

Manufacturers often insert rubber bungs in holes that would be best left open, to let water get away. This is our 100E's rear inner wing.

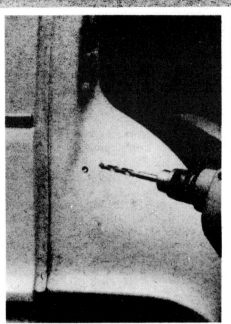

Drilling may also be required to get access into key parts of the car's structure when rust-proofing. This is a typical entry point — but watch out for an inner wall being too close to the one you've drilled for a probe to get in.

Make sure all drain holes are clear; sometimes they are hidden by a rubber seal on the door, and if blocked can actually cause several pints of water to be retained! This happened on the editorial Alfetta.

rust fluid you have chosen. Get lots in, catching the overspill from drain holes in tin cans.

The vital part of this exercise, however, is making sure you treat every possible enclosed box-section, and this requires some knowledge of how your car's bodyshell was put together. But there is no great secret to all this — just get the car on axle stands and study the construction, remembering that wherever water can get, so must your rust proofing fluid. Also look at other models like yours to see where they are rusted, so you can home in on the danger points.

Where there are no existing drain holes or other points of access (like rubber bungs,

removable light fittings, where hinges go into pillars etc, etc), drill your own — this will most likely be needed on 'D' posts and wheel arches. You can buy plastic grommets to cover the holes afterwards (paint them body colour if you like). Do not forget bonnet and bootlid frames, and doors — best of all, remove the door trims completely, though you may be able to get away with unclipping and pulling back just a part of them.

Up until now you will have kept reasonably clean — but when it comes to protecting the outer surfaces of the underside, be prepared to get filthy! This is because all traces of mud must be removed from rust-prone areas underneath, and while steam or high-pressure cleaning will get rid of the majority, you will find that the final and most vital cleaning operations will have to be carried out by hand, largely because the steam cleaner usually leaves packed dirt in wheel lips and in corners formed by chassis sections — which are exactly the places rot normally starts. The flat areas of the floorpan rarely suffer, and while these are easily cleaned, really they can be ignored.

Having got rid of all road debris, my next step on an old and rusty car is to get to work with a scraper, old screwdriver, and wire brush (hand, and on drill) and get as much rust scale off as possible; this, if anything, is a dirtier job than getting rid of the mud, and it is essential to use goggles even when using hand tools — it is all too easy to get a flake of rust in your eye. I then use a rust killer like Fertan or Trustan, or possibly an anti-rust primer like Comma's Rust Stop next, finally covering the underside with a thick wax-type sealant like Black Knight's Rust Stop, Rus-

If there aren't enough drain holes, drill them! We put an extra half-dozen in our Ford's new sills.

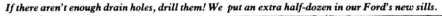

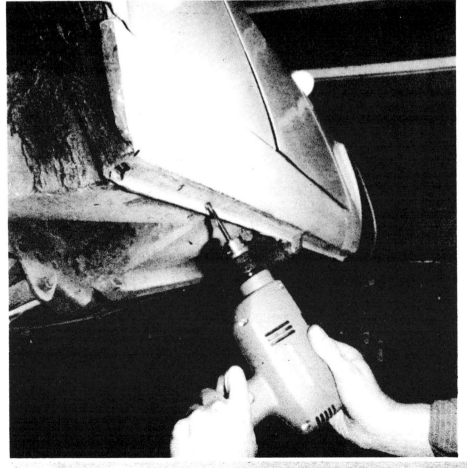

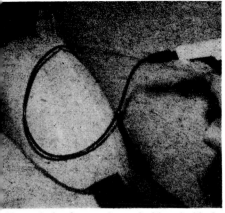

Many vital regions can be reached from inside the boot or from the engine bay; inner/outer wing joins could be tackled in this way on our 100E.

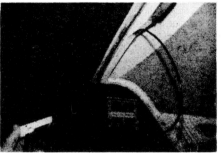

Bootlid and bonnet frames need protecting as well. After applying, close so that fluid runs into places where rain water will run later on.

tex Underbody, or the new Waxoyl underbody seal. These contain rust killers too and so can cope with surface rust not already dealt with. I reserve the use of traditional underbody seal to wheel-arch applications, where abrasion from road-wheel dirt is to be expected.

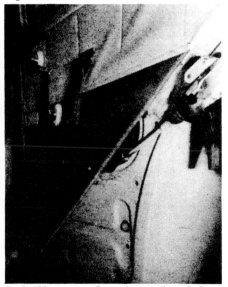

Preferably, remove door trim panels entirely so you can see condition of door and get fluid into the right places; but sometimes you can manage by unpopping just some of the clips and finding an access hole. Or drill door (on face below trigger gun in this picture).

Chassis box sections usually have holes already in them; probe extensions are almost essential to get the anti-rust waxes into their entire lengths, and take especial care to get good coverage round suspension mounting points.

The dirty part! But removal of mud build-up is crucial to preserving a car, especially when during the winter lumps like this will get saturated with salt-solution.

The Materials

We went into this topic pretty exhaustively last month, so I will not go over the same ground now; but basically, the products used fall into three main groups — rust killing chemicals, rust-killing/preventing paints, and non-hardening waxes. The effectiveness

Spring mountings are important places to clean, like the MacPherson strut anchorages of our 100E.

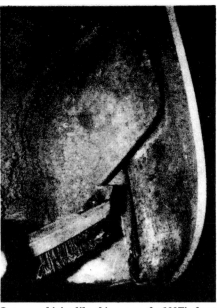

Seams and joins like this one on the 100E's front wing inside the wheelarch are highly rust-prone. Remove rust scale with wire brush.

of the first group has always been a subject for debate, and certainly the best way to counter rust is to get rid of it entirely by either cutting it out (if the metal is holed or substantially weakened), or getting the surface back to bright metal. But this is not always practical especially if you are trying to cope with, say, the entire underside of a large car.

To see how good rust preventers are, we are embarking on a simple test using mild steel plates which have been allowed to rust in the open, then lightly sanded, and the rust killers applied according to directions. The same has been done with a selection of anti-rust primers, and wax-based cavity protectors. These plates will be allowed to weather throughout the coming winter, and next spring we should have some results, along with 'before and after' colour pictures. Should be interesting . . .

Surface rust can be treated with products such as Trustan. Concentrate on corners and crevices — flat, open surfaces like the centre of the 100E's boot floor is very unlikely to rot however.

WINTER PROTECTION/Continued

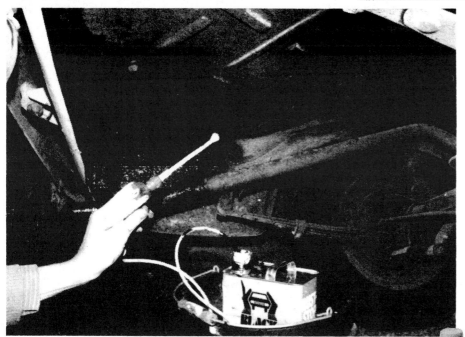

After the rust killer or primer has thoroughly 'cured', apply underbody sealant. This is Black Night's product — in common with similar wax-based sealants, placing can in bucket of hot water aids application

being runny, it pours out of every hole and onto your drive. More effective and still cheaper by about half than the 'real' thing is Shell Ensis, a rust-inhibiting oil much used by farmers to preserve agricultural machinery; you will probably have to travel out to the country and to a farm suppliers to get that, however.

The Tools

Firstly, for the underside cleaning operations you will need stiff brushes and a hose-pipe for getting rid of mud, plus a wood scraper for shifting more stubborn deposits but where you do not want to break the surface of sound underbody sealant or paint. An old screwdriver and a wire brush are essential for tackling rust scale.

For applying rust killers to large areas of metal, the quickest method is to use a trigger spray bottle, purchaseable from an ironmonger for about a quid. Use goggles and preferably a face-mask while applying materials in this way, and restrict spraying to those products which *do not* contain phos-

There are, incidentally, alternatives to the purpose-made wax-type inhibitors, which may appeal to the miserly (or the simply hard-up!). On the basis that anything is better than nothing, old engine oil poured into sills and box sections will prevent rust, but because by its very nature it disperses, regular applications — maybe several times a year — are necessary, and it is very messy because

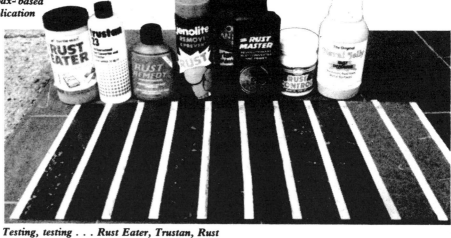

Testing, testing . . . Rust Eater, Trustan, Rust Remedy, Jenolite, Fertan, Rust Master, Rust Control and Naval Jelly applied to a test-sheet of rusted mild steel (columns on right will be used as controls). Results next year!

Traditional paint-based underbody sealants like Adup Bronze Seal should not be depised — they withstand abrasion behind road wheels very well. Incidentally, old sealant is usefully softened up when sprayed with Waxoyl etc, preventing it from drying out and flaking off.

Rust-inhibiting primers are also on test; here Kurust, Bondaprimer, Stop Rust, Beat Rust and Brown Velvet have been applied. Not shown is the test sheet for the wax-based products. All will be revealed in 1985.

The two most widely used types of applicators — the ASL pressurising pump with gun (left), and the common trigger-type (right). Both guns can be fitted with extension wands for treating box sections.

pheric or hydrochloric acid, for obvious reasons! Fertan and Trustan are safe for spraying, though do not inhale the mixture. Otherwise use a brush, perhaps with a collar made from a silver-foil dish secured with tape to the handle to catch liquid running down when applying to overhead surfaces. Again, watch out for your eyes.

When it comes to applying wax-based materials, the kits supplied normally contain either the simple trigger-gun applicator made by Cannon, or the more sophisticated ASL system whereby the container is pressurised first with a screw-in hand pump — you then control the flow of liquid from a small gun at the end of the supply line. Both types work reasonably well; the snag with the trigger gun is that your finger gets very tired when covering large areas, and the weakness (in my view) of the pressurised system is the poor control of the spray — volume is difficult to get right, and it does not shut off instantly when you release the 'button', while the spray pattern itself can be patchy. Also in my view, rarely does either piece of equipment last beyond the first period of use — even after fairly conscientious cleaning and pumping through lots of white spirit, when you come to try it again a few months later usually it does not work. A complete strip-down of the system *may* get it operational again... The root of the problem though is, in both cases, lack of real air pressure, something the amateur has to live with.

Laying-up

Once upon a time it was quite common for one's everyday car to be laid-up for the winter – goodness knows why during the period when one would get the most benefit from closed transport! Perhaps the treasured possession was reserved strictly for holidays and sunny weekends. Still, classic car enthusiasts do sometimes indulge in this activity and a few pointers cn be given.

Firstly, the engine: there are arguments for and against keeping water in the cooling

system, but personally I would go for a fresh mixture of a high-quality anti-freeze Then to prevent piston rings from rusting to bores, squirt Redex into each cylinder and turn the engine over to spread it about. Replace the plugs to stop moisture getting in, and tape up the air intake for the same reason.

It is important to change the engine oil before laying-up, as old oil contains acids which actually eat away bearings. Better still, especially if the car is to be off the road for more than a year, drain and refill with engine storage oil. This is used by the motor-boating fraternity and provides the engine with what is termed 'vapour phase protection'. This means that the oil (which has normal lubricating qualities too) gives off a vapour which perculates to all parts of the engine and prevents the formation of rust. Your garage is not likely to stock it however — go to a ship's chandlers for this item.

A sticking clutch is a fairly common complaint after some months of disuse, and while this can usually be cured by starting and driving the car in first gear, jamming the pedal down using a length of timber will stop it happening in the first place and does not appear to harm the clutch springs.

Brakes are the next biggest cause of bother. A brake fluid change (recommended once a year anyway) will help, but if the lay-up is to be a lengthy one, or your car is prone to seized wheel cylinders, your best policy is to remove each brake piston in turn and smear it and the cylinder in brake grease. Or at least, remove pads (or shoes), and pack the rubber jacket of the wheel cylinders with brake grease. The only other alternative is to change over to silicone brake fluid which does not absorb water at all, but this generally means new brake rubbers and pipes — a simple flush-through is not always effective as some conventional fluid may be left adhering to seals etc.

Damp is the big enemy of the laid-up car, so carry out the normal rust-proofing procedures mentioned previously — but coat all

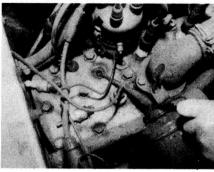

Dosing the bores with Redex prevents sticking piston rings. Redex is 'stickier' than motor oil and is thus better for this job. Vapour-phase inhibiting oil can also be used in the sump.

brightware parts with Vaseline or a wax product (WD40 only has a limited life-span). Make sure the carpets are dry, and do not forget to give the interior chrome (handles, switches, ashtray lids and so on) a light coating of Vaseline to prevent mildew. Polished engine parts can be protected in a similar way. Place the car on axle stands if you are worried about flat spots forming on the tyres — though in my experience these disappear after a few miles. But certainly, keep the tyres well pumped up if you do not take the weight off them.

Well, whether you intend using your car or not this winter, if you follow this advice there is a very good chance that it will not suffer from the onset of cold, damp weather. One thing is certain though — drive your car on our salt-laden roads for five months without taking precutions and the ravages will be great. If you want proof of that, just walk through any large car park and look at what has happened to the majority of cars more than three or four years old . . . □

Finally, you can pay to have much of your winter protection carried out for you — Zeibart have a new 'rust eliminator' treatment (shown here) for older cars, while the Danish Pava firm are willing to treat used cars too. Cost ranges from £90-£260 or more depending on car and condition.

Staff Car Sagas

Ford Prefect 100E

Paul Skilleter defends a small Ford

When the **Ford Prefect 100E's** 'rolling rebuild' was completed, there was a big rush in the PPG offices as people fell over themselves not to use it, which is why our Prefect has ended up with me for the last couple of months. I'd always wanted a company car, and anyway, I have a keen sense of pity and considered that the 100E might get emotionally disturbed if left alone in a lock-up.

It has, in fact, been very useful and June and myself have driven it a lot on local trips like shopping and collecting our five-year-old from school. Kids certainly love it, and when we give somebody else's a lift they wear a big grin all the time — much more fun than Mum's new Volvo. I have even used it — and you may not quite believe this — for travelling between my Hornchurch home and our Beckenham offices, a distance of no less than 18 miles.

However, before 100E owners get all incensed and start writing rude letters to us, I would point out that I consider the car to be very much better than some others believe. Bearing in mind that it was one of the cheapest and most basic cars you could buy, it handles and stops admirably, it's quite roomy inside, and the functional styling is, to my eyes, attractive particularly with the steel visor in place. The obvious comparison is with the Morris Minor; here the Ford is let down by its engine and three-speed gearbox, and its steering, which is much heavier than the Minor's delightful rack-and-pinion type. But it stops better and I reckon handles at least as well as the BMC product.

Yes, that gearbox — if you've ever driven a 100E you'll know that when Ford decided to make it a three-speeder, they didn't bother to alter any ratios but just left out third. So the technique to get anywhere is to rev the thing madly in second because the drop between that and top is immense — when you change up the car practically stops and you can almost hear every individual firing stroke of the engine. This makes overtaking very awk-

The Ford Prefect, minus visor shortly after its respray, in POS's driveway; a functional car, but with a certain charm.

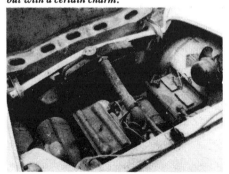

Standard 100Es aren't exactly fast, but the engine in ours, bought second-hand some months ago, seems more lacking in power than most. Note vacuum tank (left) which serves the infamous wipers.

ward, particularly if it's raining because of the 100E's other quirk, its vacuum operated

wipers — as you pull out and change into top, you have to put your foot hard down, and as this reduces the vacuum at the inlet manifold the wipers virtually stop. Then, of course, if the milk float actually decides to *accelerate* at this point, believe me you're in deep trouble.

Last weekend, and not the least because the car was coming up for sale, I gave the faithful Ford (well, it starts every time and has never let us down yet) a thorough valeting. I must say the vinyl upholstery came up like new after a good scrubbing with Decosol, and the (original) rubber mats also cleaned up very well using Solvol Black Cleaner; it's certainly a very well preserved little car, an impression reinforced when I carried out the full rust-proofing process underneath. Quite how the underside has lasted so well I don't know — maybe the first owner never took it out on salty roads. Anyway, I concluded the exercise by giving the

A few minutes with nail brush and Decosol produced a remarkable improvement to the looks of the trim, the vinyl coming up at least a tone brighter.

new cellulose a good cut and polish, and now the little car really sparkles inside and out. No doubt it will be sold by the time you read this but you could always ring the offices to see, if it has begun to take your fancy.

MAKE AND MODEL	BODY TYPE	PRODUCED	CC/CYLS	MAX. SPEED	MPG	SPARES AVAILABILITY	PRICE NEW
Ford Anglia/Prefect 100E	sal	1953-59	1172/4	71	31	✓✓	£511
Ford Prefect 107E	sal	1959-61	997/4	72	35	✓✓	£589
Ford Escort/Squire 100E	est	1955-61	1172/4	70	34	✓✓✓	£622
Ford Popular 100E	sal	1959-62	1172/4	70	32	✓✓✓✓	£494